STANSTED AIRPORT

N A T H A N   K O S K Y

S U T T O N   P U B L I S H I N G   L I M I T E D

Sutton Publishing Limited
Phoenix Mill · Thrupp · Stroud
Gloucestershire · GL5 2BU

First published 2000

Title page photograph: Nocturnal activity on
Stansted's apron. (*BAA Stansted*)

British Library Cataloguing in Publication Data
A catalogue record for this book is available from the
British Library.

ISBN 0-7509-2302-4

Typeset in 10.5/13.5 Photina.
Typesetting and origination by
Sutton Publishing Limited.
Printed in Great Britain by
The Cromwell Press, Trowbridge, Wiltshire.

*Lovingly dedicated to my wife and family
with deepest gratitude to the airmen of
the USAAF 9th Air Force 1942–5*

B-26 Marauder 42-95916 *Piccadilly Willy*. (*J.K. Havener*)

CONTENTS

FOREWORD

by

John Stent, Managing Director of Stansted Airport

From having just over one million passengers and handling around 33,000 tonnes of freight annually when Her Majesty the Queen opened our present terminal in March 1991, Stansted has grown to nearly ten million passengers and 180,000 tonnes of freight a year.

It was no mean feat to develop Stansted into the third major airport for London after years of uncertainty stretching back to the end of the Second World War. But the opening coincided with the relaxation of forty-five years of postwar traffic distribution between the London airports, the start of an economic recession in the UK and the short-term impact of a war in the Gulf, which dissuaded many people from flying. BAA therefore found itself in a situation it had never had to face before – it had to market one of its airports.

All credit must be given therefore for the determination of everyone at the airport to expand the business. Within a year Stansted had doubled its passenger traffic and ever since has achieved outstanding growth to match any other major airport in Europe.

In 1999 Stansted sought and obtained consent from both Parliament and its local community to continue to grow to the full extent of its planning permission of around fifteen million passengers per annum, which is likely to be reached in about 2005.

If the increasing demand for air travel is to be met the potential capacity of Stansted's runway has to be released. BAA believes this can be done in manageably sized portions which would be acceptable to its local community. Stansted therefore opened the new millennium by inviting its local community to join with it in looking at ways to develop the airport beyond its current planning consent.

The Stansted story is therefore far from over, and there are more exciting times ahead for the airport and those who work here. This book looks back over more than half a century of Stansted. Will the next fifty years be as eventfu? I expect they will.

INTRODUCTION

From rural village to Millennium Gateway, Stansted Airport has undergone many changes during its six decades of history. The wonderful new terminal provides its passengers with every modern travel luxury – in stark contrast to the bleak necessity of wartime Britain in which the airfield was created as USAAF Station 169.

With the world changing at an ever-increasing, and sometimes frightening, pace, it is easy to forget that it is only through the sacrifices made at places like Stansted between 1943 and 1945 that we are able to enjoy the lifestyle of the modern consumer. Stansted is perhaps unique in embodying both the fight for freedom and the many benefits victory brought. It can only be hoped that the thousands of passengers who pass through the airport every day remember, however fleetingly, the first airmen of Stansted, whose tremendous efforts made modern Stansted possible.

The many twists and turns of the airport's fate during the postwar decades have meant that on many occasions Stansted came close to being consigned to the file marked 'history', but with persistence and vision the airport is now an integral and growing part of British and European air traffic. Its design is a beacon of ingenuity and clear thought, which has placed Stansted firmly on the map and encouraged the vast growth it has attained with no detriment to passenger comfort. After some decades of struggle, the airport is now a truly excellent example of what the modern world is capable of creating.

This book attempts to record some of the images and events that have occurred in this small corner of England and give a flavour of its changing faces.

ACKNOWLEDGEMENTS

Special thanks must go to certain people who have made this book possible. Firstly, Simon Fletcher, Olwen Greany, Sarah Cook, Glad Stockdale, Anne Bennett and all concerned at Suttons, without whom I would quite simply not be an author – thank you all for your patience and invaluable help! Special thanks are also due to:

Reg Robinson, whose anecdotes and knowledge from his experiences at Stansted were instrumental in piecing together the story of Stansted's formative years, and who also allowed me access to Peter Pallet's photographic collection; Jack Havener, whose photographs and kind assistance for the wartime overview were truly an inspiration; Bob Mynn and his wonderful Buddies of the Ninth Air Force (BOTNA) organization helped me to get in touch with so many useful contacts (I can heartily recommend the BOTNA bulletin for anyone wishing to capture the flavour or get involved with the preservation of these wartime memories); John Williams, John Stent, Rona Young and Judith Slater at BAA Stansted, for their generous assistance and fabulous photographs; Adam Rowden and Richard Parker for their photography and keen help: their Stansted websites are worth visiting for ongoing information and pictures (www.aol.members.com/adamrowden and www.co35pn.demon.co.uk).

Thanks are also due to: Tony Rogers; Norman Hardman and Ron Parry at Stansted Airport Fire Service; V.J. Curtis; Lambert D. Austin and the 344th Bomb Group Association; Rebecca Travers (British World Airways); Dick Reese; William Kray; NATS Stansted; Philip Hosey and Bryan Southgate at FLS Aerospace; Peter Moon (photographer of many of the BAA pics); IWM Duxford and Lambeth; Mike Stowe at Accireports (Mike's website is at http://members.aol.com/accireport/accirpt.html); Oliver Stanek; Rita Greenberg; Luc Vervoort; Richard Davies; Edward Warburton, Michael Furze and Tony Pick at In View; Rebecca Windsor at Foster and Partners; David Garfinkel, RAF Museum, Hendon; Buzz; the *Essex Chronicle*; and all the other credited photographers and sources of advice, too numerous to mention, but hopefully you know who you are!

Every effort has been made to credit the original owner of each photograph and I apologize in advance for any oversight in this matter.

CHAPTER ONE

FROM REAPING THE HARVEST TO REAPING THE WHIRLWIND

The village of Stansted Mountfitchet, as so much of rural south-east England, was dramatically changed during the Second World War. The building of Allied fighter and bomber airfields among the rapeseed and corn provided a belligerent interlude in the tranquil setting of the English countryside. Settlements, which were previously just names on maps, became military installations of immense importance. The incongruous sight of horse-drawn ploughs and the latest in military armour going about their daily business only yards apart became an odd reality. Whereas many of these villages and towns returned to normality after the few years' service given to the war effort, Stansted's future was to change fundamentally as a result of the wartime developments in this Essex village.

With Allied bombing efforts increasing as the pendulum of attack shifted on to Hitler in the western theatre of action, the need for additional airfields became acute. The American presence in Britain required further facilities for their immense air power. The East Anglian counties were gradually overrun with an armada of aircraft, the Flying Fortresses, Liberators, Mustangs and Thunderbolts, as well as the thousands of troops, airmen and groundcrew that accompanied the war machine. This part of Britain became America's aircraft carrier as the 'Yanks' began daylight bombing operations to supplement the three years' primarily nocturnal work accomplished by the Royal Air Force (RAF) and Bomber Command.

'OVER HERE' IN STANSTED

Located only 34 miles north-east of London, Stansted Mountfitchet was chosen as the location of Station 169 by the United States Army Air Force (USAAF). As part of a 1941 agreement between Churchill and Roosevelt, Stansted and many other prospective airfields were handed over to the Americans on a 99-year lease and in July 1942 the 817th Engineer Aviation Battalion of the US army began to arrive in Essex. They started work on Stansted, bringing their mechanical diggers, rollers and machinery. The original designation was for an airfield that was to be a storage depot and repair facility for the USAAF. Like many of the wartime airfields, Stansted was to be built in a three-runway triangular layout, surrounded by a circular perimeter track to Class A standard. The main runway was 6,000 feet in length, with two subsidiary ones of 4,200 feet each.

The airfield was provisionally, and briefly, named George Washington Field. Dances were arranged to welcome the Americans in the Long Restaurant, Bishop's Stortford. The unique flavours of GI life 'over here' were to infiltrate the British way of life for the duration of the war in Stansted and in East Anglia as a whole.

With work started on the airfield, the 817th Battalion left for North Africa to be replaced by the 825th Engineer Aviation Battalion. William Kray, Executive Officer of the 825th, recalls 'When we arrived there was nothing but farmland. We pitched a tent camp in some woods adjacent to the farm and started laying out the runways.'

By the end of 1942 the four T2 hangars, Nissen huts, control tower, over forty dispersal points, operational buildings, armoury, bomb dumps and other facilities began to spring up as the base moved towards operational status. Stansted was rapidly turning into a 'state of the art' battle-ready airfield, and the largest 9th Air Force (AF) base in East Anglia.

The first recorded use of the runway was an unplanned one by a plane of the RAF. On 26 February 1943 a Short Stirling heavy bomber of 214 Squadron made an emergency landing on the incomplete and non-operational runway after returning from a raid to Nuremberg. The pilot realized his predicament once committed to landing and the aircraft overshot, striking trees at the southern end of the runway, destroying the Stirling, but not injuring the crew.

Stansted was declared operational only days after this incident and the two major units that were to grace Stansted began to arrive.

THE 30TH AIR DEPOT GROUP (ADG)

The task of the 30th ADG after its arrival at Stansted was to keep the massive 9th Air Force equipped with fully operational aircraft. Quite simply the job included repairing battle-damaged aircraft, modifying planes and weapons, and storing 'spare' bombers to use as replacements. This operation took place on the south side of Stansted's runway (near where the new terminal is situated today). The facilities were pronounced as the 2nd Tactical Air Depot once the airfield was officially designated in October 1943.

The 30th ADG arrived from San Antonio, Texas, and were assisted throughout their stay at Stansted by various Mobile Repair and Reclamation Squadrons. Their job was to 'pick up' damaged and immobile aircraft from the vicinity in order to relay them to Stansted for repair by the 30th ADG. The Group was highly successful and crucial to the war effort waged against Germany. Although the fighting squadrons take much of the spotlight for their efforts during these years, the work of the groundcrews as well as units such as the 30th ADG based at Stansted cannot be overstated in ensuring that enough aircraft were airworthy at all times.

THE 344TH BOMBARDMENT GROUP (MEDIUM)

The US 9th AF activated the 344th Bombardment Group (BG) on 31 August 1942. They were immediately equipped with the controversial Martin B-26 Marauder medium bomber. The group was designated a training unit and based at MacDill Airfield, Tampa, Florida, where they stayed until transfer to Lakeland late in 1942.

The B-26 was considered a fearful aircraft by many of the training pilots. First flown in 1940 the B-26 design won a US government contract to be a '300mph bomber'. The Marauder was initially the scourge of inexperienced pilots thanks to its need for high speed landings (130 mph), and outstanding flying skills owing to its alleged small wing area not providing as much lift or control as other contemporary aircraft. MacDill was therefore the scene of several accidents and even despair as the Marauder earned such nicknames as 'widow-maker' during the 'blood and guts' training of the 344th. At several junctures even the US government had their doubts over the success of the aircraft despite her debut performances in the Pacific.

However, after perseverance and with some skilled trainers who had faith in the B-26, the rookies of the 344th gradually mastered what was turning out to be a good aeroplane. At Drane Field, Lakeland* the 344th honed their skills at take-off, assembly, and formation as well as simulated bombing missions, using Florida's rail marshalling yards as practice for those that waited in Europe. Finally, after much speculation as to their ultimate destination, in the opening months of 1944 the 344th BG was transferred to England.

Comprising the 494th, 495th, 496th and 497th Bomber Squadrons and under the command of Colonel Reginald Vance, the group arrived at Stansted between 20 and 24 February 1944. The B-26s were camouflaged drab olive green with a grey underside but, after hearing that it was possible to gain an extra 3mph of speed, some pilots chose to remove the grey paint from beneath the planes before arrival in England. This revealed the shiny bare metal of the B-26 and the group became known as the Silver Streaks. Their motto, which they belligerently bore, was 'We Win or Die'. On arrival, the group began training and geographical familiarization while settling in to their new Nissen hut accommodation at Stansted. The small huts usually had eight bunks along either side with a footlocker at the end of each bed. The harsh British winter must have seemed a rude awakening to pilots trained in the Florida sun and who had been on the African continent only days before.

The German welcome was no friendlier. On their first night, Lord Haw-Haw, the infamous propaganda radio announcer, welcomed the 344th personally and kindly reminded them of the perils of warfare. Stansted was never far away from the front line with intruder missions and V bombs a regular occurrence. Lambert D. Austin writes: 'Each night for several weeks, the raiding planes of the Luftwaffe flew across our field on their way to bomb London or industrial plants at Chelmsford, the detonation and flashes of their bombs making the latter place appear to be just on the fringe of our field.'

The B-26's initial forays into the European Theatre of Operations (ETO) some months earlier had been a disaster. Despite only small success in the Pacific at low level, the top brass sent the B-26s of the 322nd Bombardment Group, based at Bury St Edmunds, to Ijmuiden, Holland, to bomb the submarine pens at low level on 17 May 1943 on only the second B-26 mission in the ETO. All ten aircraft failed to return, hit by deadly flak or attacking Me109 fighters. This proved a lesson in the making of the B-26's ultimate success as she reverted to bombing from higher altitude where the accurate Norden bombsight and the aircraft's performance would be most advantageous. By the time the 344th had arrived at Stansted, other 9th AF Groups had determined that medium bombing with a formation of two boxes of eighteen aircraft was the most successful means of using the Marauder and its 4,000lb bombload.

After a number of orientation flights and a diversionary mission, the 344th finally went into combat on 6 March 1944. The target was Bernay St Martin airfield in France.

* The 344th shared the facilities of Drane Field with the 407th Fighter Gp, who flew P-51 Mustangs.

There were no casualties and only four of the thirty-seven aircraft were damaged by flak. The target was accurately hit. The group received a commendation on its second mission the next day. With the realities of war, this excitement was bound to be short-lived. The next day, 8 March, saw the first casualties as two Marauders collided in thick cloud, killing all the crew.

Over the coming months, however, the Silver Streaks almost daily pounded targets in the occupied countries of northern Europe. Wearing their distinctive group markings of 36-inch high white triangles on the tail and the codes K9, Y5, N3 and 7I for squadrons 494 to 497, the 344th quickly gained a superb reputation along with the Marauders of the 9th AF as a whole.

Increasingly, the group's missions became a vital prelude to D-Day. Bombing of airfields and targets such as coastal defences, railway bridges and marshalling yards was designed to render any counter-attack to D-Day less effective as part of Eisenhower's 'Transportation Plan'.*

The group had only lost a small number of aircraft in the early months but had a notably bad day on 28 May 1944. Bombing a bridge in Paris, five aircraft were lost to flak, with thirty-one crew posted as missing or killed. Four of the aircraft were from the 495th Squadron. These lives were not lost in vain as the 344th led what was arguably to become the most important operation of the war only nine days later.

D-DAY

Lt Col. Lucius B. Clay described D-Day as 'the day we had been preparing for, bombing for, and training for, the past six or seven months'. The 344th was chosen to lead the 9th Air Force's B-26 force in a crucial pre-landing attack on the beach fortifications in Normandy. With the new black and white 'invasion stripes' freshly painted, and with the call-sign 'Pawnbroker', the 344th set off in the early hours of 6 June 1944 – the entire 9th Air Force followed the Stansted squadrons on that day!

The rapid painting of the now legendary invasion stripes was an unenviable task. Airman and groundcrew member Dick Reese remembered, 'If you consider the size of the aircraft and each stripe being 2 feet wide times fifteen airplanes it's an immense assignment. The paint alone half-filled a small truck. Brushes were in all sizes, the local stores sold out. I thought it was a dumb idea thought up by some general . . . was I wrong!'

The Marauder's mission, along with the whole of the Allied bomber force, was to destroy Rommel's 'Atlantic Wall' of defence in preparation for the landings on Utah Beach. The B-26s were once again asked to fly as alarmingly low as 500 feet. Taking off from Stansted at 0412 hours, 495 Squadron's Mary Jo skippered by Major Jens A. Norgaard led the way and headed for the coastal batteries on the Cherbourg peninsula, despite the miserable weather. The 9th AF attacked the beaches of Beau Guillot, La Madeleine and Martin de Varreville just after 0600 hours while other groups hit comparable targets along the beaches. The Marauders each dropped sixteen 250lb general-purpose bombs. The payload of the B-26 had often been four 1000lb bombs but this would have meant a danger of bigger explosions knocking the low-flying aircraft out

*The Transportation Plan was to disrupt fuel, supplies and troop movements in France as much as possible so any prolonged response to the Normandy invasion would be hindered by a lack of basic fighting requirements.

of the sky. The smaller craters made also allowed better 'foxholes' for advancing troops to take cover in when landing on the beach. Drops were also made in the water to destroy the metal obstacles the Germans had embedded offshore.

Despite the failure of many D-Day plans, the Marauders of the 9th AF were able to paralyse or stun the defences on Utah Beach just as the hundreds of landing craft containing the thousands of troops approached below. The briefing had suggested a 'milk run' (easy mission) with little resistance but Sergeant Ray Sanders in *Terre Haute Tornado* described the flak as 'the most withering, heavy and accurate we ever experienced'.

Despite a second mission on 6 June to Amiens, the 344th BG lost only one B-26 on that momentous day: Second Lieutenant James B. McKamey's aircraft was hit by flak and exploded in mid-air over the Channel.

Colonel Robert B. Witty was later awarded the Distinguished Flying Cross for his performance in the lead plane on D-Day at the Normandy Beachhead and with a combination of skill and bravery the Marauders of Stansted performed a crucial role which saved countless lives.* The men and machines of the 344th BG had forever etched Stansted's place in history.

PUSHING BACK HITLER

The 344th continued to provide valuable support from Stansted to the Allied advance through France. Mission numbers averaged over one per day in the ensuing weeks, continuing the focus on choking the German supply chain by hitting bridges, fuel dumps and railways and provided close ground support for Allied soldiers by attacking defended towns, German troop strongholds and gun emplacements. After the first V bombs landed on English towns on 12 June 1944, and even 'buzzed' over Stansted itself, the Marauders hit back at the launch sites only days later in 'Operation Noball'. The 344th were now able to see a more direct result of their good work.

The 344th BG received a coveted Distinguished Unit Citation (DUC) for its valour between 24 and 26 July 1944. During these days the group had knocked out a crucial bridge at Tours le Riche, bombed Nazi troops at St Lô and attacked a viaduct at Maintenon before heavily damaging a fuel depot at Semonches. The DUC was recognition of the important role the 344th was having in Europe's liberation.

INTO EUROPE FOR THE 344TH

As the Allied forces advanced, the days of the 344th at Stansted were numbered; by the end of September 1944 the Marauders had to move nearer the advancing battlefront. The group received orders to relocate to airfield A-59 at Cormeilles in France. As quickly as they had arrived in Essex, the Silver Streaks departed for the continent and the final push for Germany; boxes were packed, trucks were loaded and sent to the south coast for shipping or put on the Dakotas for aerial transport (the first cargo flights from Stansted?).

During their seven-month stay at Stansted the 344th had dropped over 7,739 tonnes of munitions, flown over 140 missions and aided in preparation and execution of arguably the most momentous battle in history.

---

*One of the main reasons cited for the heavy loss of life on Omaha Beach was the failure of the B-17 force of the 8th AF and the naval bombardment to destroy gun emplacements. The B-17s flew higher than the B-26s attacking Utah and were thus hindered by cloud.

Their heroic and intense work continued until VE-Day, their raids penetrating far into enemy-held territory, over Germany's railways, troops, supply centres and airfields and even helping the victory at the Battle of the Bulge. The 344th progressed further into Europe during this period and ultimately occupied Schlessheim near Munich once hostilities had ended.

By the end of the war the 344th had undertaken 266 missions in 14 months and had been the most accurate Medium Bomb Group in the 9th Air Force in 1944. Stansted was left with an indelible link with European history and the great air war that had taken place.

STANSTED LEAVES THE FRONT LINE

The USAAF used the airfield as a storage area for the 8th AF. A detachment from the massive Burtonwood Base Air Depot Area arrived in late 1944 to oversee the arrival of factory-fresh bombers and fighters. Once again, Stansted could be seen littered with B-17s and other US machines awaiting repair or orders to join a squadron as replacements.

The pace of life at Stansted slowed considerably now the Allies were on the offensive and front line action became more distant. By August 1945 all aircraft stored had either been flown on to their squadrons or 'disposed of'. It is likely that even brand new aircraft were broken up, being obsolete or surplus before they had even been used in anger.

Stansted's runways were left tarred and sanded and daubed with white crosses to indicate closure. The future of the airfield, as with so many across Britain, now lay in considerable doubt despite Stansted making such a vital contribution when only three years earlier there had been nothing but meadows and farmland. These years, however, proved to be only the belligerent and glorious start to a more enduring story.

Curious locals get their first glimpse of the USAAF's somewhat awkward arrival. Here, the 850th Engineers attempt to manoeuvre some of their heavy equipment through the narrow streets of Stansted village by the crossroads at Chapel Hill. Note the old LNER sign for Stansted station on the right. (*Merton Marshall via the Peter Pallet Collection*)

The foundations are laid as the frame of a T2 hangar rises from the soil. The rural backdrop was to be changed forever as a result of this building work by the 850th EAB. (*Peter Pallet Collection*)

A USAAF engineer poses proudly by his all-terrain tractor during a break from work. (*Peter Pallet Collection*)

Lieutenant Morton Schlesinger was determined to marry his English fiancée in September 1943, even when he lost his leg in an accident while laying the concrete runway at Stansted. Schlesinger refused to allow this setback to interfere with his big day, and so, still in his wheelchair, Morton married Rita, his English girlfriend of eleven months, in Braintree military hospital only days after sustaining his injuries. As the couple were Jewish, the local paper reported the event as 'a ceremony that combined the age-old rites of the Hebrew religion with the atmosphere of modern war'. The happy couple returned to America once Lieutenant Schlesinger had recuperated and they remained together until his death in 1997. (*Rita Schlesinger-Greenberg*)

Opposite: One of Stansted's T2 hangars undergoing intensive building work by the 850th EAB and their machinery in 1942. These hangars were eventually to house the B-26 aircraft that were based at the airfield. Each bomber squadron based at Stansted was assigned to one of the hangars, while those on the southern side were occupied by the Air Depot. Some of them are still in use today after nearly sixty years. (*Peter Pallet Collection*)

Two British soldiers watch as a bemused British 'bobby' has his photo taken with a Stansted-based American airman. Amazingly, American tourists still crave such souvenirs to take home! The George Inn was situated on the corner of High Street and North Street in Bishop's Stortford. (*Peter Pallet Collection*)

Below: Loss of life was not unknown at Stansted, even before the first combat squadron had arrived. The wreckage of a North American P-51 Mustang, a replacement aircraft prepared by the 30th Repair Squadron, lies at the perimeter of the airfield after crashing on 13 December 1943. Lieutenant John E. Cerutti witnessed the crash; he claimed that he heard a crack before seeing the plane falling to earth without its tail section. The pilot, Second Lieutenant Isaiah J. Goldberg, was fatally wounded. (*USAF*)

As well as constructing the airfield, the 850th EAB took part in helping Britain further, and on a more personal basis. Members of the battalion clubbed together to sponsor one of Britain's growing number of war orphans as part of the 'Stars and Stripes War Orphans Fund' run in conjunction with the Red Cross. Participation in this worthy scheme helped highlight to the men the cause they were fighting for, as well as endearing them to their British hosts. In March 1944 the 850th 'adopted' a nine-year-old girl called Colleen B., whose parents were known to have died in the blitz. Before the guys met Colleen, they were moved from Stansted to Oxfordshire in preparation for post-D-Day work. A search for Colleen's whereabouts was mounted by the 850th in 1990. Note the tented accommodation behind the sign in the top photo, evidently taken before the living quarters were completed. (*Peter Pallet Collection*)

CERTIFICATE OF GOOD WILL

The "Stars & Stripes" War Orphans Fund

Colleen B. —
Born 6th Oct. 1935

850th Engineer Aviation Batt...
Selected March, 1944

Fund Administered by the American Red Cross
"Stars and Stripes" War Orphans Fund Committee

Commissioner
American Red Cross

E. M. Llewellyn Lt Col
Editor
"Stars and Stripes"

The quartermasters of the 850th EAB, complete with chef's headgear and utensils hung up in the background. In the middle of the front row is Sergeant Al Akers, the oldest serving soldier in the entire US armed forces. He had actually fought in the First World War, and pleaded personally with the President to let him serve his country once more. President Roosevelt consequently signed a special order allowing him to go to Europe as a non-combatant member of the USAAF. He was placed in charge of cooking in the 850th Battalion. (*Peter Pallet Collection*)

Sometimes the damage sustained from enemy guns meant landing wherever possible. Here B-26C 41-34683 from the 322nd BG, based at Andrews Field in Essex, rests after making a wheels-up landing at Stansted at dusk in December 1943. Thankfully no one was injured; indeed, all bar the pilot and co-pilot had parachuted from the plane prior to landing. (*USAF*)

As with so many USAAF bases, the troops in England were entertained by some of the finest and most popular Hollywood stars of the day. In 1943 both Frances Langford and Bob Hope (above) performed here as part of a welcome to the EAB working on Stansted. Such visits to Allied troops by celebrities served as a tremendous morale-booster throughout the war and helped to keep the servicemen motivated. (*Peter Pallet Collection*)

Before being sent to the European Theatre of Operations (ETO), crews were fully trained up on the unique intricacies of flying the B-26. Such operational training was often hazardous because novice pilots found the Marauder a difficult aircraft to fly, resulting in a number of accidents. Here pilots take part in formation practice at Lakeland Army Airfield (Drane Field) in Florida. (*J.K. Havener*)

The badge of the 344th Bomb Group, with their motto 'We Win or Die'.

After the sunny climate of Florida and a lengthy journey via Brazil, Liberia and Morocco, the 344th BG arrived in March 1944 to find England gripped by winter. Here the first occupants of Hut 10, in the 497th Squadron area at Stansted, put their sheepskin flying jackets to good use in the British snow. Standing, left to right, including: Hollinger, Wroneski, Healy, Borreson. Kneeling: Havener, McLaughlin, Horn, Nemeth. (*J.K. Havener*)

Captain R. Wilson sits proudly in his B-26, named after his home town, Terre Haute in Indiana. *Terre Haute Tornado* flew 114 combat missions, mostly as lead aircraft. She also flew 80 straight missions without an abort for mechanical problems. Despite this rich history, she was stripped and blown up for scrap along with all other European Tour B-26s in 1946. (*J.K. Havener*)

The 344th BG suffered its first casualties on its third mission. On 8 March 1944 two B-26s – 42-95926 piloted by Captain Jack Miller and 42-95981 flown by First Lieutenant John Eckhert – collided while climbing into formation above North Weald for the mission to Soesterburg, Holland. The two planes emerged from thick cloud on an unavoidable collision course. Such situations could prove just as hazardous to the pilots as flak or enemy fighters. All twelve crew members were killed. (*USAF*)

Colonel Reginald F.C. Vance (left) and Captain Lucius B. Clay Jr leaning on an Army Air Force jeep in front of a Marauder hardstand. Vance was Commanding Officer of the 344th Bomb Group at Stansted until he was transferred to take over command of the 99th Bomb Wing in November 1944. Clay went on to command the 344th after the group left England for Europe. The absence of D-Day stripes on the bombed-up B-26 confirms that this photo dates from April 1944. (*BAA Stansted*)

The Martin Company implemented several innovations in their Marauder medium bomber. One of these was that the B-26 was the first aircraft to have an all-Plexiglas nose-cone for the bombardier's position, defended by a machine-gun. *The Buzzard* was badly damaged in August 1944 during a costly raid on Brest harbour. (*J.K. Havener*)

The half-olive, half-natural metal finish and a pilot called Captain R.W. Maffry combined to give this aircraft its name: *Maffry's Mottled Marauder*. The line below reads 'The Wings are Coming by ATC' – a humorous remark prompted by the fact that the Marauder was deemed difficult to fly, partly owing to its small wing area. Experienced pilots, however, proved the design to be highly successful. Indeed *Flak Bait*, of the 322nd BG (based at Great Saling), was the first Allied bomber in Europe to fly 200 missions. (*J.K. Havener*)

A tight formation of five Martin Marauders from the 344th BG at Stansted attacking the railway marshalling yards at Namur in Belgium on 10 April 1944. This was the group's thirteenth combat mission and the smoke billowing from the clearly visible target suggests a successful raid. The 344th dispatched thirty-eight aircraft which dropped 152 1,000lb bombs on Namur. The B-26 was the first combat aircraft to be built with an all-electrical bomb-release mechanism; this provided far greater reliability and therefore enhanced the productivity of Marauder raids. On that day the 344th was in the thick of the action; also bombing gun batteries at Le Havre and Le Clos on the French coast. (*USAF*)

Officers relax in the 497th Squadron barracks, outside the amusingly named 'Hut too thee fo' – drill practice was still fresh in the memories of these airmen! Despite the USAAF's excellence at providing all available luxuries for its servicemen, this officer clearly preferred the comfort of a British army sweater, which may well have been procured in a friendly trade. (*J.K. Havener*)

In April 1944 engine failures forced the pilot of B-26C 41-34723 to make a belly-landing in a hayfield in East Hanningfield, Essex. The aircraft was carrying eleven people at the time – it was ferrying personnel, including a technical inspector from the Martin Aircraft Co., for the 30th Repair Squadron of the 30th Air Depot Group based at Stansted. None of the occupants suffered major injuries. For ferrying duties the B-26 had turrets, guns and armour plating removed. (*USAF*)

A Marauder of the 496th Squadron, 344th BG, attacks the day's target on 22 May 1944. Much of the later part of this crucial month was spent knocking out the Luftwaffe's aerial power, communications and coastal defences ahead of the imminent D-Day invasion. This mission was no exception as 42-107552 joins in the strike on Beauvais-Tille airfield, probably with eight 500lb demolition bombs. No losses were sustained in the day's raids but seventeen aircraft were damaged. Ironically, Beauvais-Tille was later to become home to the Marauders of the 322nd BG after the invasion of France. (*USAF*)

The view from a B-26 over the 497th Squadron area at Stansted in May 1944. It is easy to see how the array of Nissen huts, administrative buildings and runways dominate the previously sleepy Essex farmland. The brief appearance of such airfields in the English countryside was a feature of rural East Anglia during the Second World War, but Stansted's aviation status proved somewhat more enduring than most. (*George Kammermeyer*)

Martin Marauders were usually crewed by six men – pilot, co-pilot, bombardier, navigator, engineer and radio operator. Add a painted lady to the six crewmen and there is no better name for this Stansted B-26 than *Six Hits and a Miss*. Sadly the original photograph did not include all of the '*Six Hits*'. (*J.K. Havener*)

The original control tower was of standard construction. These towers were built on the many airfields used by the USAAF in Britain. Stansted's tower remained in use, after modifications, well into the 1980s. (*BAA Stansted*)

Facsimile – allegedly named because it was shot up so much that it was a mere facsimile of a Marauder – finally came to grief on 27 April 1944 when bombing the Fort Mardick coastal defences. *Facsimile*, piloted by Lieutenant Alton B. Rubin, was one of two planes shot down moments after releasing their bombs. Only two parachutes were spotted as the aircraft spiralled fatally to the ground. (*J.K. Havener*)

The B-26B was defended by eleven .50 calibre guns: one in the Plexiglas nose; four under the fuselage belly; two in the first ever power-operated dorsal gun turret; two in the waist; and two rear-firing guns in an electric-hydraulic turret. Combined with a maximum speed of over 300mph, these guns gave the B-26 as much immunity to enemy attack as possible. Out of just under 130,000 B-26 sorties in the ETO, only 911 Marauders were shot down and destroyed. (*J.K. Havener*)

'Jocko' was a strictly forbidden friend picked up during the 344th's stopover in Liberia on their journey to England. The monkey became a mascot to the airmen after they swapped its sunny home for that of a bewilderingly cold Essex winter – brass monkeys indeed! (*J.K. Havener*)

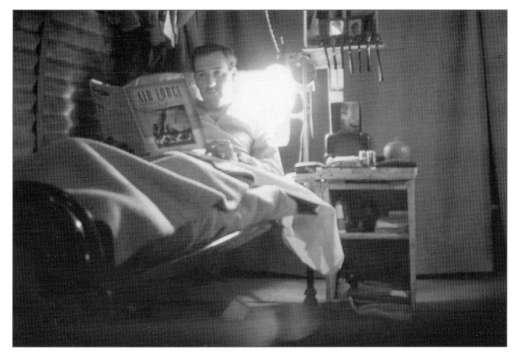

Stansted's wartime living quarters. Pictures of his loved ones and a row of pipes sit among the personal belongings of Jack Havener as he takes in some background reading in the 'comfort' of his bed. Stansted Mountfitchet was regarded as something of a state-of-the-art airfield, and living conditions were comfortable if a little more spartan than back home in the USA. (*J.K. Havener*)

The Hearse III, piloted by First Lieutenant Young, pictured at Stansted in April 1944. The overalls strewn on the concrete belong to a member of her groundcrew. A fuel truck drives along the perimeter in the background. There were two package guns on either side of the fuselage: the B-26 was the first aircraft to use such weapon pods. The pilot operated the guns via a button on his control wheel. (*J.K. Havener*)

Rum Buggy, serial number 4295924, was another of Stansted's Marauders. It was crash-landed by Captain Al Frieberger on 26 May 1944 at nearby Great Dunmow airfield after being shot up on a raid on Chartres airfield, France. Tail-gunner Bob Dahlem was wounded. The replacement B-26B was named *Rum Buggy II* – crews often retained the names of lost aircraft in this way. (*J.K. Havener*)

As with all Allied bombing missions, the need to take off and form up as quickly as possible required 'massed' take-offs and maximum precision. Here about a dozen 'Silver Streaks' are visible as they trundle towards the runway in May 1944. Although it was severely frowned upon to allow the B-26s to leave the tarmac taxiway, it seems haste got the better of some pilots – tyre tracks in the grass leaving their evidence! (*J.K. Havener*)

You Cawn't Miss It! was a joking reference to the English turn of phrase when giving directions. Clearly certain differences in culture and language caused amusement among the visiting GIs. This is Captain Ashberry's B-26, pictured near Stansted's perimeter, waiting for the bombs ready on their racks to be loaded up for the day's mission. (*J.K. Havener*)

A 496th Squadron crew, led by Captain R.W. Maffry (second left), pose in front of *Maffry's Mottled Marauder*, probably in April 1944. The flying jacket worn by the crewman on the far right bears the motto 'No Shack – No Sack'. Shack, in bombing terms, meant a direct hit. This bombardier was clearly trying to remind himself that if he didn't hit the target he would be losing his sleep ('no sack') thanks to some extra practice sessions! (*BAA Stansted*)

You've 'Ad It was another contemporary British phrase picked up on by USAAF airmen, and this time used to name First Lieutenant W. Harrison's Stansted Marauder. Clearly, it was the artwork rather than the name adorning 42-95952 that grabbed the attention of those in the 497th Bomb Squadron! (*J.K. Havener*)

Baggage handling, 1944-style! Here, bombs are being prepared for their journey to occupied Europe on a 497th Squadron dispersal in May 1944. Groundcrews loiter by the munitions as they await orders to 'bomb up' their aircraft. The B-26 Marauder could actually carry a 4,000lb bomb-load – considerably more than its American medium bomber contemporaries, the A-20 Havoc and B-25 Mitchell. (*George Kammermeyer*)

The venerable *Rosie O'Brady*, pictured here after twenty-six missions had been notched up on her fuselage. Airman Richard Reese was tasked with painting some of the 'nose art' on to the Stansted Marauders, including that of the famed *Rosie*. He recalls that he was paid $10 for the job! Other aircraft that bore his handiwork included *Mary Jo*, *Merry Jerry*, *Barracuda* and *Mary Sue III* (the aircraft flown by the CO, Colonel Vance). After the war Reese graduated as an advertising designer from the University of Philadelphia. (*Dick Reese*)

The idiosyncrasies of Britain clearly seeped into the lives of the USAAF servicemen stationed in East Anglia during their three-year stay. Smartly dressed and riding the ubiquitous standard issue bicycle, First Lieutenant John Hollinger of the 497th Bomb Squadron stops to enjoy his fish and chips purchased in nearby Bishop's Stortford. (*J.K. Havener*)

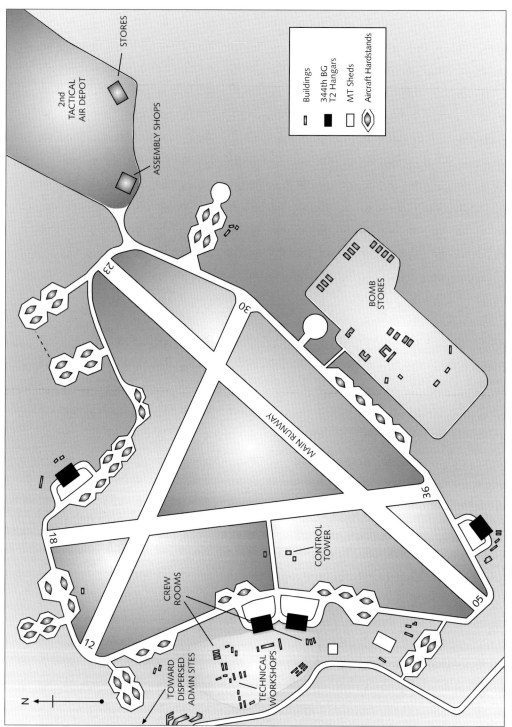

Basic layout of Stansted as a USAAF base between 1943 and 1945. The modern terminal would sit roughly where the 2nd TAD area was situated. Only the main runway is in existence today.

This B-26B of the 495th Squadron, *Shopworn Angel* 42-95917, belly-landed at Stansted in the spring of 1944. It actually belonged to First Lieutenant Henry 'Woody' Woodrum, but as he was on leave in London Captain Lucius Clay borrowed it. Unfortunately, thanks to spirited German defences, Clay didn't quite return it in the same condition in which he found it. On 28 May 1944 Woodrum and his crew, flying another B-26, were shot down during an attack on a bridge near Paris. It was a bad day for the 344th BG: thirty-one crewmen were recorded as missing in action on that day. *Shopworn Angel* was lost in action on another costly day for the 344th: Valentine's Day 1945. It was one of six aircraft lost. (*J.K. Havener*)

Yo-Yo Champ was so named because she just kept coming back (the bomb tally on the fuselage pays homage to that). The pilot A.J. Wood was caricatured in the fluffy chick! (*J.K. Havener*)

Above: Bishop's Stortford High Street during the war. The sleepy Essex village was the haunt of off-duty GIs based ten minutes away at Stansted. Airman Richard Reese recalls his impressions of 'a quaint, quiet town of farmers, small businesses and well-stocked dark-wooded pubs. We met the people and the pubs right quick!' (*J.K. Havener*)

Two airmen, Taub and Taylor, stage a good-humoured fight over the right to care for the 'bathing beauty' which adorned the side of this B-26, *Valkyrie*, of the 497th Bomb Squadron. It was not unusual for the crews to paint voluptuous ladies on their aircraft, but a fully naked one was more of a rarity. As a result this B-26 proved popular among photographers until it was destroyed in a take-off crash in January 1945. (*Dick Reese*)

Terre Haute Tornado pictured after suffering minor flak damage, highlighted by co-pilot Havener. It was more serious on 20 June 1944, however, during a raid on V-1 launch-sites in northern France, when flak wiped out her left engine, rudder cable and undercarriage tyres. Heroically Captain Wilson managed to complete the bomb run and nursed *Tornado* home to England, landing at RAF Manston in Kent. (*J.K. Havener*)

This USAAF Percival Proctor was involved in an unusual incident at Stansted on 3 June 1944. Swerving to avoid oncoming cyclists on the taxiway, it skidded and hit a parked car! The pilot was reprimanded for taxiing too fast in an aircraft with poor visibility and the aerodrome patrol was also ordered to be more careful with traffic on the perimeter track. The Proctor was used for administrative duties by the 2nd Tactical Air Depot based at Stansted. (*USAF*)

Bunny's Honey was the aircraft of Lieutenant-Colonel Emanual Schifani, the 495th Squadron's Operations Officer, who went on to receive a Distinguished Flying Cross in November 1944. The markings on the mission tally are more complicated than most: the duck symbolizes a diversionary mission, the doughnuts are aborted raids, and the candy sticks are missions where no bombs were dropped. Groundcrew chiefs often added their names to the nose-wheel door of 'their' planes. (*J.K. Havener*)

Crews relax in the 497th Squadron officers' living area. The Nissen huts were standard buildings, and hundreds of them were scattered across the many USAAF airfields in East Anglia. The officers are, as ever, immaculately dressed despite their 'off duty' status. The man on the right, leaning on the bicycle, is Pilot John Nemeth, who flew a Marauder called *Johnny Come Lately* (see p. 45). (*BAA Stansted*)

Groundcrew pose in front of *Mary Jo*, the lead plane of the entire 9th Air Force on D-Day. Sadly, lead bombardier Captain James P. Parish, the oldest and one of the most popular flying officers at Stansted, was tragically killed when *Mary Jo* was struck by a single piece of flak no bigger than a ten-pence coin. The tiny fragment pierced the Plexiglas at speed and Parish was killed instantly. (*Dick Reese*)

The view from the cockpit – two boxes of Marauders in flight. The D-Day invasion stripes visible were hastily painted on by groundstaff for the big day. The unit marking or large white triangle on the tailfins made the 344th highly distinctive in flight. (*J.K. Havener*)

Doubtless posing for publicity purposes, these four pilots gather beside the nose wheel of a B-26 Marauder to plot their imaginary mission as other 344th personnel on the base cycle past unaware! The line-up includes Jack Jones (left), Richard Cliff (centre left) and W.R. Hunter (far right). (*BAA Stansted*)

Lead ship takes to the sky! The 344th BG favoured gaining altitude as quickly as possible after take-off rather than trying to pick up ground speed. Note the undercarriage is already retracted, although the aircraft has only been airborne for a matter of seconds. (*J.K. Havener*)

My Colleen had flown over thirty missions when she came to grief after a raid on Argentan in France on 7 June 1944. After taking a direct hit in the left engine, Captain 'Father' Hynes coaxed the B-26 back to England on one engine and with no hydraulics. She crash-landed on Stansted's grass, adjacent to the runway. The aircraft was written off but all the crew survived, with no serious injuries. (*J.K. Havener*)

Four formations of Stansted Marauders are a fearsome sight in the clear sky. Fresh D-Day stripes adorn the aircraft – this photo was taken only four days after that momentous occasion. The 497th Squadron, pictured here on 10 June 1944, was continuing to support the Allied advance into France by attacking road junctions in the Normandy town of St Lô. (*George Kammermeyer*)

First Lieutenant Jewell Maxwell, the first Commanding Officer of the 496th Squadron, named his personal B-26 *Maxwell House*, using the slogan borrowed from the coffee of the same name. Maxwell's distinguished career in the USAF saw him rise to the rank of major-general after the war, and his last duty was to oversee the now defunct Air Force supersonic transport programme. (*J.K. Havener*)

It was important for personnel of the 344th to unwind when not on duty. Here men play volleyball in the officers' area of the 497th Squadron. The building in the background was the shower hut for officers; the tower contained the water tanks. (*BAA Stansted*)

To celebrate American Independence Day on 4 July 1944, all the personnel of the 344th BG took part in a bicycle race around the camp at Stansted. In the centre is Colonel Reginald F.C. Vance, the 344th's Commanding Officer. On his left are Lieutenant Hamden (497th Squadron) and Lieutenant Stokes (496th Squadron.). As well as competing in a bike race, the 344th also managed to bomb a bridge at Oissel on that day. (*BAA Stansted*)

Marie II after crash-landing in July 1944. Note the absence of the nose-gun: perhaps the bombardier ditched the heavy .50 calibre machine-gun in order to reduce the weight of the stricken aircraft. The well-worn paintwork of *Marie II* is ample evidence of the 66-mission tally etched on to the fuselage. (*George Kammermeyer*)

This B-26 of 496th Bomber Squadron crash-landed as a result of a training flight error on 8 July 1944. Slowing the plane after landing, pilot Joseph S. Danner called for the flaps to be raised. However, the novice engineer accidentally moved the landing gear handle to the 'up' position instead, causing the Marauder to slide to rest on one wingtip. (*USAF*)

Jack Havener proudly displays his A-2 jacket, freshly personalized with the name of his aircraft, *Terre Haute Tornado*. Sergeant Wojack, from the 497th Squadron's communication section, was responsible for much of the 'jacket art'. Havener stands by the 497th's rather bare volleyball court. (*J.K. Havener*)

Captain Schwaegerl (standing, right) of Cleveland, Ohio, and his crew pose in front of their aircraft on 1 August 1944. On that day these young men undertook the bombing of a railway bridge at Bouchemaine. (*BAA Stansted*)

A popular photo opportunity for 344th BG personnel named John! *Johnny Come Lately* was the aircraft of Captain John J. Nemeth. According to its nose tally, this venerable B-26 had racked up over 125 missions; the bomb fins painted red represent missions undertaken after D-Day. This picture was taken after the 344th departed Stansted for mainland Europe. (*J.K. Havener*)

A veteran of well over a hundred missions, *Hard to Get* lived up to her name. She was flown by the CO of the 497th Squadron, First Lieutenant Delwin D. Bentley. Bentley's association with the Marauder cannot be exaggerated – he was initially appointed as a training instructor in the American operational training bases and his abilities in this role, and later in combat, showed sceptical crew the true capabilities of the B-26. Such was his faith in the plane that he once simultaneously feathered both props on a training flight, much to the disbelief of all concerned. After a distinguished career in the air force, Bentley passed away in 1992. (*J.K. Havener*)

Squadron Operations Officer First Lieutenant Daniel Brawner awards the Purple Heart medal to First Lieutenant Leo Fenster, a bombardier/navigator. He was wounded when a flak shell exploded in front of his plane, shattering the Plexiglas nose; Fenster suffered severe cuts. (*J.K. Havener*)

Bombardier Irv Johnson was shot down over occupied Europe but evaded capture by the German army thanks to the help of underground resistance forces. Here Johnson smiles gratefully after his miraculous return to Stansted in August 1944. (*George Kammermeyer*)

The invasion force fly by at Stansted. In September 1944 the Allies swooped to recapture Holland and the Low Countries. Stansted saw the invasion force at first hand when the skies were filled with dozens of gliders and their tugs taking troops across the sea to liberate occupied Europe. The Allies were firmly on the offensive now. (*J.K. Havener*)

Dozens of B-17 Flying Fortresses and P-51 Mustangs can be seen parked along Stansted's 'smaller' runways and dispersal areas. During Stansted's time as a BADA storage depot towards the end of the war various American types such as P-47 Thunderbolts, B-24 Liberators and even P-61 Black Widow night-fighters occupied the base. The aircraft awaited dispatch as replacements to active squadrons. The current terminal is now situated at the top right of the main runway. (*BAA Stansted*)

A line-up of seven factory-fresh B-17 Flying Fortress bombers in storage and under guard along the taxiway. The bombers had been moved over from Ireland and packed tightly into Stansted as the threat of enemy attack receded now the Allies were on the offensive. Previously parking the aircraft in such close proximity was deemed to create too much of a tempting target for the enemy. (*Peter Pallet Collection*)

CHAPTER TWO

THE UNCERTAIN CALM

As soon as the USAAF left Stansted, the eerily quiet airfield was turned over to RAF Care and Maintenance with the 263rd Maintenance Unit (MU) arriving in August 1945. It was their task not only to process the unwanted materials and equipment that were now surplus to requirements, but also to dispose of hardware from fifteen other nearby RAF stations. Many of the RAF airfields in the locality were now earmarked for closure with the land destined to return to agriculture, and even Stansted had no foreseeable permanent role.

The airfield's appearance became somewhat ragged thanks to the 800 tons of surplus equipment moving through the station each week. Help in this ongoing process was provided by 400 resident German prisoners of war (PoWs). They were allowed a relatively free rein now that the war was over, restricted only by a 20-mile radius of movement. Indeed, three PoWs actually played for local football team Stansted Rovers in the Spartan League from August 1945.

Stansted's aviation activities at last recommenced late in 1946 when the London Aero and Motor Services (LAMS) moved their fleet of Handley Page Halifaxes from Elstree when the tiny airstrip proved unsuitable for the ex-RAF bombers. Indeed, one of the aircraft was lost on take-off at Elstree. With Dr Graham Humby at its head, LAMS began their Stansted charter services in December; because of the primitive civil facilities they not only had to provide their own Air Traffic Control and emergency services, but customs procedure meant stopping off at Heathrow for clearance.

Despite these quirks, commercial flying at Stansted was under way and by 1947 LAMS was flying to destinations like Iceland, North America and Australia, as well as regular fruit collection from Italy. Their services expanded when they linked up with South African airline Alpha, which operated both passenger and freight charters from Johannesburg, which LAMS now benefited from.

By this time, the RAF's presence was in decline at Stansted with much of the disposal work done. They began a series of sales, which saw the RAF auction off thousands of tons of surplus materials.

Meanwhile a second private operator joined LAMS at Stansted. Kearsley Airways received a DC-3 Dakota in late 1947 flying its debut trip in November to Delhi on a charter on behalf of BOAC. Soon World Air Freight Ltd made it three airlines at Stansted, but they moved on to Bovingdon. Kearsley, however, were to make the most notable contribution of the three to the history of Stansted when they were one of the first civilian airlines to assist in the 'Berlin Airlift', making 246 sorties during 1948 from Fassberg, Lubeck and Fuhlsbuttel using two DC-3 Dakotas.

LAMS' life span proved to be all too short when it ceased trading in July 1948.

Although Skyflight took over some of the LAMS aircraft and services, even Skyflight only extended the life of the Halifax operations until May 1949.

Stansted's future passed through the first of its ongoing crossroads when the ever-changing fate of London's airfields was decided for the first time of many! The government determined that Stansted had lost out to Gatwick as the official overflow for the newly developed Heathrow; Blackbushe was given the role of diversionary airfield. Despite this setback, Parliament ordered £30,000* to be used to upgrade the airfield's facilities and maintain the runway so there seemed some cause for optimism.

Another long-term resident at Stansted, the Ministry of Civil Aviation Flying Unit, which carried out calibration and airport instrument checks, arrived in 1949. They originally used Avro Ansons and were to remain at Stansted for a number of decades, utilizing such aircraft as Airspeed Oxfords and a Chipmunk in the early years.

Stansted's importance had been marginalized since the war and the departure of the USAAF. Kearsley was the only major operator at the turn of the decade, but even they ceased flying in 1950 and concentrated on aircraft engineering. However, events were to take a positive and unexpected turn in the early part of the 1950s.

SERVING THE EMPIRE

1951 saw an increase of traffic and the Lancashire Aircraft Corporation (LAC) moved its fleet of Avro Yorks from Bovingdon to Stansted, having taken over the operations of Skyways (while retaining the Skyways name). William Dempster Ltd who flew tourist flights to Johannesburg soon joined them, using Avro Tudors.

Stansted's movements now included several test flights. One of these notoriously ended in disaster when a Handley Page HP88 broke up above the runway killing the pilot, Squadron Leader Broomfield DFC, who is buried at St Mary's Church in Stansted. The Radlett-based Handley Page, however, went on to turn the embryonic aircraft into the successful Victor bomber. This incident highlighted the inherent dangers of test flying to the daring pilots of the era.

Trooping flights around the Empire saw Stansted's passenger footfall increase substantially during the early 1950s. As well as the seventy or so freight flights which now flew from the airport, airlines such as Skyways began to profit from global troop movements to and from places such as India, Singapore, the West Indies and Africa. Another frequenter was Prestwick-based Scottish Airlines, using the airfield as its English outpost for yet more trooping. The increased movements meant increased incident. One such tragedy occurred when a Skyways Avro York went missing en route to Kingston, Jamaica.

Stansted became the temporary home of the Battle of Britain Air Display in 1952 and 1953 with such delights as F-86 Sabres, Meteors and Canberras of the RAF, a Dassault Flamant from France, an Avro Tudor, and even a Dragon Rapide giving joy-rides.

By 1953 the Ministry of Aviation had again taken stock of the seven airports still active around London. Stansted's future development looked limited for the second time when once again Gatwick was chosen for further development as the major international airport, second only to Heathrow. Stansted was deemed the 'wrong' side of London and stunted by the large amount of traffic still occupying the East Anglian skies from nearby United States Air Force (USAF) and RAF bases. Stansted was only to be kept open until Gatwick's development had been completed, at which time the airport faced likely closure.

---

* The USAF, who still maintained the upkeep of the airfield as part of its lease, reportedly paid for the £30,000 upgrade.

The airport's destiny was salvaged and even shaped for the future by a bizarre turn of events that occurred while the government cogitated late in 1952. With the Korean War still fresh in American minds the USAF wanted to make provision for the possibility of a Europe-based war against the Soviets. Stansted was chosen to have its runway lengthened in order to facilitate a modern American bomber base for the US Strategic Air Command.

The 803rd EAB brought the USAF back to Stansted in numbers for the first time since their departure almost a decade earlier. The main runway was to be extended to the north-east by another two-thirds. It was to be one of the largest runways in Great Britain – a total length of 10,165 feet (over 3050 m) – in order to be a main standby base for the NATO forces' heavy bomber fleet.

Once the work started, civilian passenger flights still utilized the new main taxiway as a runway in order to land and take off thousands of passengers during the three years of construction. Indeed, over 52,000 passengers used Stansted in 1955 alone, more than double the number using Gatwick at this time.

The military flavour at Stansted, again created by the US barracks and servicemen, was enhanced by the arrival of 99 F.4 Sabre fighters between 1955 and 1958. The USAF had loaned the jets to the RAF as an interim replacement for the soon-to-be delivered Hawker Hunter. The Sabres passed through the hands of Aviation Traders, Freddie Laker's engineering company, who were awarded the task of overhauling the jets and returning them to USAF markings.

Once the improved runway was fully completed in April 1957 the USAF 3928th Air Base Group handed over control to the British government. Within two years, despite all the work and expense, Stansted was already written off by the powers that be at NATO as somewhere to be used only in extreme emergency.* However, the 10,000-foot legacy, left once again by the Americans, was to be a defining factor in shaping Stansted's future.

The late 1950s saw the resumption of trooping and charter work from the now extraordinarily large Stansted runway. Such flights kept the airport active and ensured that it continued to operate flights to destinations such as Singapore, Cyprus, Malta and Australia; Skyways operated trooping flights to the Suez region during 1953 and 1954. Passenger numbers, however, dipped to around the 20,000 mark once the North Terminal at Gatwick was opened in 1958.

Such changes saw Scottish Airlines cease to fly from Stansted in 1958 and some of Skyways' scheduled services moving on to the larger Heathrow in 1959, but Air Charter increased their use of Stansted and introduced the Bristol Britannia to their fleet. The Britannia was one of the last great turboprops produced in the face of the dawning age of jet airliners in the 1960s.

As the close of the decade approached, with a still relatively quiet circuit at the airport, BEA decided to undertake major crew training operations with the potential of at least more aircraft movements arising from this initiative. The airport had moved on since the war. Britannias and Constellations had replaced Dakotas and Halifaxes. The runway and other airport facilities had advanced beyond recognition and were, in hindsight, well placed for greater progression. The future was still uncertain, but the longer Stansted avoided closure, the more important it was likely to become for Britain's increasingly busy skies.

---

* Bizarrely, Stansted still remains a theoretical 2nd line NATO airfield until its lease to the USAF expires in 2041.

London Aero & Motor Services Ltd (LAMS) was the first pioneering airline to use Stansted for commercial services late in 1946. LAMS used the former wartime bombers for freight services until the company went into liquidation in the spring of 1948. LAMS none the less holds a unique place in Stansted's history. Handley Page Halifax G-AIWN, *Port of Darwin*, was used as a civil freighter until being broken up in 1950 and is pictured here parked on the southern side of the runway near where the Compass base and Diamond hangar are now situated. (*Peter Pallet Collection*)

Kearsley Airways was the second airline to operate services from the Air Ministry-owned Stansted. Flying Douglas DC-3 Dakotas and a Percival Proctor, Major J.W. Kearsley began using the airfield as a base for the movement of refugees and various cargoes. Kearsley also linked Stansted to another important piece of history when the airline became one of the first private airlines to take part in the Berlin Airlift in 1948. Today Kearsley's business involves the maintenance and servicing of components at Stansted. (*Peter Pallet Collection*)

Canadian operator Lome Airways leased this Avro Tudor (G-AKCA) from Surrey Flying Services, who operated at Stansted from 1951. The Tudor was returned to the airport after its spell in Canada and remained static for several years until it was eventually broken up at Stansted in July 1959. Another Tudor, G-AGRY, a former Air Charter plane, sits behind in the breaker's yard, also destined to be scrapped. (*Peter Pallet Collection*)

Trooping flights were a major part of the airport's movements throughout the 1950s. This Avro York C.1, pictured in front of the control tower, served with 51 Squadron during its military career. Later registered G-ANVO, the York was operated by Skyways and used serial XJ264 when on troop ferrying duties from Stansted. (*Peter Pallet Collection*)

A BOAC Avro York pictured at Stansted in September 1950. Named *Milford*, this was one of ten Yorks bought from BOAC by the Lancashire Aircraft Corporation in 1951, and operated from Stansted. Their new owner often used them for trooping flights. *Milford* was one of the last Yorks in existence when it was eventually broken up at Luton in November 1963. The York was the transport development of the legendary bomber, the Avro Lancaster, and bore many design similarities. (*Peter Pallet Collection*)

Opposite: A poster advertising the air display at the airport, organized by the RAF Association in September 1953. The day's programme included flying displays by Meteors of 601 Squadron from North Weald, Canberras of 617 Squadron from Binbrook, and USAF Thunderjets, which were then based at Wethersfield in Essex. Spectators were also invited to climb aboard an Avro Tudor – what an unlikely treat this would be for today's aviation enthusiast! (*Peter Pallet Collection*)

Royal Air Forces Association (Stansted Branch)

Registered Under the War Charities Act 1940

AIR DISPLAY

AT

Stansted Airport, Stansted Mountfitchet,

ESSEX

Saturday, September 26th, 1953

By kind permission of the Minister of Civil Aviation

FLYING BY **JETs** OF THE

R.A.F., R.A.A.F., R.A.F.V.R., R.C.A.F., U.S.A.F., and Civil

Individual Aerobatics and Formations, Pleasure Flights,

STATIC EXHIBITION:

Aerial Survey Photographs, Jet and Piston Engines,
Demonstrations of Flight Radio Aids,
Tudor Air Liner open to Inspection,

Fire Fighting Demonstration — Numerous Other Attractions

St. John Ambulance Brigade in Attendance — Refreshments

Licensed Bar by RAYMENTS of PELHAM 1.30 – 5.30

Airport Open 12.00 noon. — Flying Commences 2.00 p.m.

Admission : Adults 2/- — Children 1/- — Car & Occupants 10/- — Motor Cycles 5/-

Frequent Bus Service from Bishop's Stortford and Stansted to the Airport

Dance to FREDDIE WILSON'S BAND

7.30 to 11.30. — Licensed Bar — Admission 3/-

The second USAF base at Stansted was set up to house troops of the 803rd EAB whose job it was to extend the runway to its present length. The task was completed by 1957, although the opportunity for Stansted to return to its former status as a bomber base lasted only two years. The soldiers' huts were rather more comfortable than the Nissen hut accommodation of the Second World War. The American design of postwar hut was on 'stilts' and therefore raised from the ground. On the left a soldier poses under the boast of 'World's Best Engineers'! (*Peter Pallet Collection*)

A South African-registered Tropic Airways' Avro York on a trooping visit to a wet Stansted. The RAF had previously operated this particular York. (*Peter Pallet Collection*)

Air Charter was one of the few regular operators using Stansted in its fledgling years. Originally based at Bovingdon and Croydon, Air Charter used ten Avro Tudor aircraft converted by Aviation Traders into 'Super Traders' from 1956. This airline had also taken part in the Berlin Airlift from Stansted in 1952. Tudor Super Trader G-AGRG *El Alamein*, seen here loading, was destroyed only three years later when she caught fire on take-off at Brindisi, Italy, in 1959. (*Peter Pallet Collection*)

American heroics at Stansted continued into the 1950s when US Army servicemen stationed at the airport rushed to help trapped passengers injured in this major incident on 22 September 1954. These dramatic pictures show Scottish Airlines Avro York XG898 after it skidded and crashed on take-off, breaking its back, as it embarked on a trooping flight to Malta. The US GIs quickly brought cranes to the scene as poisonous fumes and the threat of an explosion put the trapped passengers in danger. Unfortunately, despite the rescue team's good work, two people were killed in the accident. (*Stansted Airport Fire Service*)

Aviation Traders' ATL.90 Accountant was a Freddie Laker design for the business market produced at Southend in 1957. Although the prototypes were never put into full production, many of the innovations were incorporated into later production aircraft. (*Peter Pallet Collection*)

A Skyways Lockheed Constellation protrudes its distinctive tail-plane from one of Stansted's wartime hangars. Skyways of London began operating from the airport in 1959, when they used it as a base for crew training. They later went on to fly scheduled flights to Mediterranean destinations such as Malta and Cyprus. Euravia purchased Skyways in 1962. Note the wartime constructions to the left of the hangar; the water tower for what was probably a squadron showering facility is still visible. (*Peter Pallet Collection*)

Britavia operated Handley Page Hermes G-ALDI for trooping flights after purchasing the aircraft in 1954. This four piston-engined Hermes had only a twelve-year lifespan before it was broken up at Stansted, superseded by the turbo-prop and jet-engined generation of airliners. (*Peter Pallet Collection*)

A converted and glorified wartime hut served as the original terminal building for many years, emphasising Stansted's relative 'backwater' status in those days. The waiting area in the 1950s and 1960s was not quite the hub of activity and shopping that can be seen today! (*BAA Stansted*)

CHAPTER THREE

STANSTED IN THE 1960S – PROGRESS AND PROTESTS

The 1960s began rather ominously at Stansted with Air Charter the only airline basing their regular operations from the airfield. Freddie Laker, the owner of Air Charter, also moved his Aviation Traders production base of Carvair DC-4 conversions to Stansted. The ATL.98 Carvair capitalized on cheap fuel, making it as cheap to fly a car across the English Channel as it was to take the ferry. Each conversion had an enlarged hold in the nose and could carry eight to ten cars and their occupants. The first Stansted-built Carvair flew in 1962 and over the course of the 1960s Aviation Traders delivered the type to airlines such as Aer Lingus, Channel Air Bridge, British Air Ferries, Ansett ANA and Aviaco of Spain. A pair remain operational today.

Air Charter quickly found the 1960s a decade of change when it was merged into the newly formed British United Airline (BUA). Laker was still at the helm, and BUA continued to use Stansted as a base for global trooping activities. Helped by the now active BEA pilot training programme, Stansted was becoming slightly busier in flying terms. Indeed, BEA churned out three hundred newly qualified pilots from Stansted each year, using Vickers Viscounts and Vanguards, Argosy, Tridents and DH Comets. Passengers passing through the airport numbered 59,000 in 1960.

A new arrival on the non-airline side was the Ministry of Aviation Fire Service Training School, which set up a new base at Stansted after moving from Pengham Moor in Cardiff. The school utilized the former USAF church as a main lecture hall and it was to be an enduring part of Stansted's framework for more than two decades, before moving on to Teesside Airport. Many thousands of firemen passed through their induction at Stansted, resulting in the rather interesting sight of old airframes lying burnt out along the airfield's perimeter after use in practice drills!

THE BIG JET ACE LANDS
Stansted's oversized new runway was designed to take multiple-engined military jets, but in 1961 KLM announced that it intended to take advantage of this asset for civil purposes. The Dutch national carrier was to use its DC-8 jets on transatlantic routes to America, the pioneering service commencing in March 1961 to New York Idlewild Airport (now JFK Airport). This first passenger jet flight was a true landmark in the history of the airport. KLM paved the way for the likes of Capitol and Canadian Pacific, who in the succeeding years added charter flights from Stansted across the Atlantic to

destinations such as Los Angeles and Calgary. The year 1961 proved to be a period of progress, and not just on the jet front: Lloyd International and Cunard Eagle began charter services from the airport and at last Stansted became an important base for traffic movements around London's skies.

The year 1962 saw the ailing Skyways taken over by Euravia, which operated to various continental destinations using Lockheed Constellations previously run by Skyways. Euravia went on to become Britannia Airways after acquiring a fleet of Britannia prop-liners. Now based at Luton, Britannia is still at the forefront of charter aviation in Britain and its aircraft can still be seen operating from Stansted today.

Despite steady years of increased footfall through the airport, a period of negative upheaval was only just around the corner. BEA transferred its training base to Shannon and Malta, while BUA lost its main trooping contract to Hong Kong. On the credit side Channel Airways began to fly from the airport. This meant that once again there were no regular scheduled services from the airport, only charter work and crew training by the likes of BUA on their VC-10s. Stansted's most notable service was that of accommodating diversions from Heathrow.

Simultaneously, however, important developments seemed to be taking place in the airport's favour when the government announced in March 1964 that Stansted was to become the much-needed third airport serving London. At a cost of millions Stansted was to be upgraded in order to take in the overflow from Heathrow and Gatwick that was expected to take place early in the next decade. Immediately there was a local uproar: people were alarmed at the prospect of up to four runways, with houses under threat of demolition to make way for the proposed 19 square miles of airport tarmac, not to mention the impact of noise pollution in such a rural area. Stansted was still a relative backwater in comparison to London's 'big two' and the possibility of the suggested upgrade into an airport of similar proportions saw the local protest group up in arms. The battle was to develop over the coming years. . . .

CONTINUED INCONSISTENCY

Lloyd International began to grow during the 1960s, sending cargo out to the Far East as well as IT charters to and from Scotland in the latter part of the decade, but once again there always seemed to be a counterbalance to any growth. Overseas carriers Braathens SAFE, Capitol and Canadian Pacific all moved their charters to Gatwick, where the facilities were better. Indeed, Stansted was still using wartime Nissen huts for its lounges and terminals. This deficiency was highlighted when diverted passengers were sometimes obliged to stay on board their stranded airliners as the airport simply could not cope! In 1966 the British Airports Authority (BAA) assumed control of Stansted, and acknowledged that the need for upgraded facilities was crucial if Stansted were to survive. In 1965–6 fewer than 4,000 passengers used the airport: Stansted's future as a viable concern was once again in the balance.

Following BAA's appointment, passenger handling responsibilities were hived off to Avia, which replaced BUA. The airlines responded and from a low point in 1966, movements slowly increased thanks to the likes of LTU and its fellow German airline Condor. The Ford Motor Company, which had its headquarters at Brentwood in Essex, also set up a base at the airport to operate corporate and technical staff flights in 1967. Ford used the former Scottish Airlines T2 war-era hanger and utilized a Nissen hut as an office. The Ford fleet initially consisted of a single Grumman Gulfstream, but it would grow in the coming years and the usage of the airport proved to be a major boost to movement figures during this time.

Despite the pressing need for action over the issue of the third London airport, the government was facing a difficult situation. After a two-year public inquiry in 1965–6, a White Paper was published in May 1967. This reported that Stansted had great advantages over any other proposal, through a combination of the large modern runway already in place, existing air traffic control logistics, and easy passenger access from London. The go-ahead was given for the investment of £47m into the multi-runway airport and twenty thousand jobs were proposed. The inquiry had looked at eighteen sites but Stansted was 'the only one with a clear prospect of making a successful third London airport'.

However, the Essex residents once again mobilized in the face of noise and concrete encroachment into their rural peace and much controversy arose over the merits of the plan. Despite BAA Chairman Peter Masefield's assurances that Stansted would actually benefit the area, Essex County Council issued a writ trying to halt the impending development – and Parliament backed it. The matter was even debated in two television documentaries. Never in all its history had Stansted received so much attention – even if it was not all positive!

In October 1967 the government was forced to take a backward step in the face of vehement opposition by slowing down the timetable of development and subsequently realigning the runway layout in order to change the flight paths of future air traffic. This was followed by confirmation that Stansted's development would be altered to minimize noise nuisance around Harlow, Sawbridgeworth and Bishop's Stortford. In February 1968, with redevelopment just around the corner, the residents were given a further massive boost when the President of the Board of Trade, Anthony Crosland, announced in the House of Lords that a new public inquiry would reassess the viability of other sites. This was known as the Roskill Commission and was set up as a direct result of public fears over the enlarged Stansted; the area's residents had forced a gradual climbdown.

Despite this apparent blow to the future growth of the airport, the archaic facilities were still replaced by a terminal built in 1968–9 at a cost of £200,000. This at least seemed to secure some sort of future for Stansted while the Roskill Commission deliberated. The approval of night flights in 1968 also went some way to increasing Stansted's role and simultaneously incensed the local residents once again!

After the mid-1960s slump Stansted's business continued to grow steadily. Channel Airways had moved in from the smaller Southend Airport its entire fleet of BAC 1-11s and Tridents flying IT charters to many European holiday destinations. Channel also introduced the first domestic scheduled flights service from the airport when it flew Vickers Viscounts to Jersey, Guernsey and Scotland. The hundred flights a week from Stansted's busy new resident as well as various ad hoc charters helped to lift passenger numbers back up to considerably over the 100,000 mark in 1968 and gave the airport new purpose.

Transmeridian's arrival from their former base in Cambridge brought a new operator to the airport, and their all-cargo fleet of Canadair CL-44s and Douglas DC-7s became a regular sight at Stansted. Along with Lloyd's increased cargo operations to Rotterdam and the Far East, the airport could now boast a growing concern in London's aerial freight movements. Simultaneously, Aviation Traders rolled out its last Carvair freighter from the airport.

Servisair took over the role of handling agents in 1968 in preparation for the expected growth and improved modernization of Stansted. The control of baggage movements and restocking of aircraft provisions are duties they continue to fill to this day. Channel soon ordered ex-BEA and Olympic Airways Comets to augment their fleet, keeping Servisair busy as the decade drew to a close.

At last, in 1969, the new terminal opened on the northern side of the airport not far from the 344th BG hangars. It was not exactly as had been planned for much of the decade but none the less it was a vast improvement. When thirty-five aircraft were diverted from Heathrow in December 1969 Stansted was at last able to cope with the demands of increased traffic – this would provide a vital step in the airport's journey to becoming London's largest aviation hub.

Despite the new optimism for Stansted, in 1969 the Roskill Commission produced a short-list of four sites for the proposed and long-awaited new airport. Stansted was conspicuous by its absence. Once again the decade closed with no definite plan for the airport, although now it was a more active airport (219,000 passengers in 1969) with a modern terminal. Stansted was now busier and of greater importance than at any other stage in its civilian life. This provided a strong foundation for growth and the hope that a period of stability could now make Stansted a permanent fixture.

One of the most widely used airliners in the immediate postwar decades was the Douglas DC-3 Dakota (designated the C-47 by the USAAF). Thousands of these venerable twin-engined transports were released by the armed forces after hostilities had ceased and they became a common sight at the world's airports. Stansted was no exception. This Dakota worked for Standard Telephones & Cables until it was sold to South Africa in 1974. Amazingly, this elderly DC-3 still flies commercially for Debon Air in South Africa as ZS-PTG. (*Peter Pallet Collection*)

Bristol Britannia G-ANCE of British United Airways (BUA) awaits its passengers. It had previously served with with Air Charter Ltd, until their fleet merged into BUA in 1960. Freddie Laker, the owner of Air Charter Ltd, became managing director of the new airline. They operated several trooping flights every week from 1960 to 1964 before losing the government contract. (*Peter Pallet Collection*)

The arrival of the inaugural scheduled DC-8 in March 1961 was an important first for the airport. KLM ran a service to New York using a Douglas DC-8, the precursor of the new generation of transatlantic airliners. Here the resident baggage handlers await *Thomas Alva Edison*'s maiden arrival as she taxies from the runway, and (below) the passengers board for the America-bound flight. (*Peter Pallet Collection*)

An early Fokker F.27 Friendship at Stansted, 17 May 1961. This aircraft, which was one of the first of the 100 series to be produced, was operated by the National Iranian Oil Company for executive usage and was named *Pazanun*. It was bought by the Swiss operator Balair, but was subsequently damaged beyond economical repair after a very heavy landing at Malaga in 1964. (*Peter Pallet Collection*)

After a civil career that included stints with United Airlines and Northeast Airlines, the Ministry of Aviation in 1962 purchased this 1956-built Vickers Viscount for use by the Empire Test Pilots School. Re-registered XR802, and seen here opening throttle on the taxiway, she flew for another ten years before being broken up. (*Peter Pallet Collection*)

Stansted-based Skyways was the first airline to receive the successful HS.748 in 1962 and its aircraft appeared regularly at the airport until Skyways merged with Dan-Air London in 1972. G-ARMX was eventually donated to Manchester Airport Fire Service after a 28-year flying career. (*Peter Pallet Collection*)

Stansted was home to the Civil Aviation Authority's Fire Training School for many years until its departure to Teesside Airport in 1981. The school trained over nine thousand firemen from around the world during its tenure at Stansted and many old airframes were used for practice emergencies for the fire crews. (*BAA Stansted*)

A Bristol Britannia accelerates along the runway at Stansted in the early 1960s. This Britannia was part of the Cunard Eagle Airways' fleet (latterly known as British Eagle); common visitors to Essex, their operations included a weekly flight to the Adriatic holiday resort of Rimini in Italy. The airline was owned by Harold Bamberg in April 1948 and it became one of the more service-oriented charter operators over the next twenty years. They were widely renowned as one of 'Europe's finest independent airlines'. (*Peter Pallet Collection*)

Aviation Traders, owned by Freddie Laker, had the ingenious idea of converting twenty-one regular DC-4s into specially designed freighters, which were renamed Carvairs. New nose sections were built at Southend Airport and attached to the fuselages at Stansted throughout the 1960s. The conversion had the effect of speeding up the plane by 5 knots, as the extra weight on the front of the tail-heavy DC-4 resulted in a more balanced design. This particular example is one of the very last in existence; it is now owned by Great Arctic Airways in America. (*Peter Pallet Collection*)

The engines of this Douglas DC-4 were being stripped down at Stansted in the mid-1960s. Ace Freighters' livery depicted this aircraft as the ace of spades! G-APEZ was sadly broken up in 1968 after a 22-year lifespan. (*Peter Pallet Collection*)

Canadian Pacific Douglas DC-8-43 taxies along Stansted's tarmac in July 1964. This airline flew services between Stansted and Calgary for a few years before moving its operations to the better-equipped Gatwick airport. CF-CPI *Empress of Calgary* served Canadian Pacific for over a decade, ending her days as part of the Opa-Locka Fire Dept in Florida. (*Peter Pallet Collection*)

As with all airports, accident response procedures need to be rehearsed on a regular basis. The presence of the Fire Training School at Stansted made this an even more regular occurrence. This Trans Meridian DC-7 cargo plane makes a useful prop for the staged emergency. (*BAA Stansted*)

For over two decades Stansted's facilities remained somewhat spartan. Wartime Nissen huts housed the departure and arrival lounges, restaurant and administration offices until the erection of a more modern terminal in the late 1960s. Note the post-box adjacent to the passenger building, pictured here in May 1967. (*Peter Pallet Collection*)

This Handley Page Herald D-BEBE of Bavaria Fluggesellschaft often visited British airports before it was sold to the Israeli airline Arkia soon after this photograph was taken in 1967. BAC 1-11s carried out Bavaria's Munich operations after the sale of the Herald. (*Peter Pallet Collection*)

Echoes of Stansted's past arrived in 1967 in the shape of a pair of former-USAF Douglas A-26 Invaders. Both a contemporary and a successor of the B-26, the Invader served for many years in the US forces. N190Y was one of two owned by Occidental Oil Co., and it is pictured here during a visit to Stansted for servicing. (*Peter Pallet Collection*)

Trans Meridian leased this Douglas DC-7 and began operating their fleet from Stansted in the late 1960s, remaining until 1980. G-ATAB's four Pratt & Whitney radial engines seem to be undergoing servicing, as the cowling on the far side of the aircraft has been removed and laid out on the tarmac. These sturdy engines ensured that the DC-7 had a range of over 4,000km, which they needed for flights to Africa and the Far East. (*Peter Pallet Collection*)

A major incident at Stansted in the late 1960s involved Lloyd International's Bristol Britannia 312 G-ADVS, which suffered an undercarriage collapse on landing. Part of Lloyd's Far East operations, the aircraft was eventually repaired and returned to service. (*Stansted Airport Fire Service*)

The Sud/Aerospatiale Caravelle was a common visitor to Stansted during the 1960s and early 1970s. In all, 282 examples of this French medium-range airliner were produced and arrived at Stansted in the colours of several airlines, including Iberia and Finnair. These two Sterling-liveried jets are being fuelled up before departure. (*BAA Stansted*)

BEA's Comet 4B G-APMF being used for crew training at Stansted. Named *William Finlay*, this aircraft served BEA for over ten years before a brief stint with Dan-Air. She was finally broken up at Lasham in 1976. (*Peter Pallet Collection*)

A Lloyd/Donaldson Britannia 317 on the apron at Stansted in April 1968. At this time Lloyd International used Stansted as a base for various routes including cargo flights to Hong Kong, charters to North America, and Inclusive Tour (IT) flights from Glasgow. The Ford hangar can be seen on the left and the wartime control tower is situated on the right. (*George Pennick via Peter Pallet*)

On 4 December 1967 there was a major accident at Stansted, amazingly without loss of life. During a crew training exercise, the BEA Armstrong-Whitworth Argosy G-ASXP failed to gain height on take-off and came down hard adjacent to the runway, narrowly missing a taxiing De Havilland Dove. Although the Argosy caught fire and much of it disintegrated, the cockpit area with the occupants safely inside was thrown clear. (*Stansted Airport Fire Service*)

This Boeing 707-355C *Prins Bernhard* was operated by the Dutch airline Transavia for only five months of its long and distinguished career. It is pictured here at Stansted on 4 August 1968, after which British Caledonian operated it for several years. Indeed, records suggest that this aircraft is still in use over thirty years later by International Air Tours of Nigeria. Note the wartime buildings still scattered around on the far side of the runway. (*Peter Pallet Collection*)

A Tellair Bristol Britannia parked next to a Canadair CL-44 operated by Transmeridian, pictured at Stansted in 1968. Aviation Traders' (ATEL) staff can be seen servicing the airliner in preparation for its departure. (*BAA Stansted*)

BUA ceased its passenger operations at Stansted in 1964. Its Gatwick operations, however, continued until BUA merged with Caledonian in 1970. BUA had still used Stansted for crew training on its VC-10 fleet until this time. The VC-10 was tremendously popular with pilots and some still serve in the RAF today. G-ASIX went on to serve with Air Malawi before being preserved at Brooklands Museum. (*Peter Pallet Collection*)

A line-up of jets on the tarmac. A Channel Airways' Vickers Viscount and a Saturn Airways DC-8 are the main planes in view. Saturn operated transatlantic flights from Stansted for a period in the late 1960s and early 1970s. During the same period Channel was responsible for much of the airport's increased footfall – they operated up to a hundred flights per week at their zenith. (*Peter Pallet Collection*)

Channel Airways' BAC 1-11 G-AWEJ pictured outside one of the 1943-built T2 hangars. Channel was one of Stansted's major operators in the late 1960s before its bankruptcy in 1972. This aircraft served with Channel from 1968 before going on to a distinguished career with British Airways. Note the old terminal being constructed in the background; it was finally opened in June 1969. (*BAA Stansted*)

Saturn Airways' Douglas DC-8 N8995U descends over the perimeter fence after another transatlantic crossing, September 1969. This veteran airliner is still part of United Parcel Service's fleet over thirty-two years after she was built. (*BAA Stansted*)

Behind the mysteriously placed VW Beetle car sits a Trans Caribbean Douglas DC-8 on a visit from America. N8786R *Barbara Henry II* was delivered new to Trans Caribbean in 1967 and served until 1971 when the company merged into American Airlines. This aircraft was eventually converted into a freighter and still operates for United Parcel Service. (*BAA Stansted*)

CHAPTER FOUR

SLOWLY TOWARDS A MODERN STANSTED, 1970–88

The 1970s saw a positive movement across the entire aviation industry towards jet transport. Stansted was no exception: Channel Airways bought a DH Comet from BEA while Lloyd International began using a pair of Boeing 707-321s. By 1970 Ford's corporate fleet also expanded with the addition of an HS.125, and became of increasing importance to the airport, accomplishing more than 2,100 flights in 1970. The majority of these flights were to Valencia, Liverpool, Ford's European headquarters at Cologne, and to a new factory in Marseilles. Stansted's passenger aggregates for 1970 were up to over half a million – an amazing advance from the mere 4,000 in 1965/6. In addition to passenger movements there were 27,291 training flights around the Stansted circuit, making the airport a very busy place and contributing to a profit of £75,000 for the 1970/1 financial year.

The year 1971 saw the first of a new breed arrive on the tarmac at Stansted. On 8 February BOAC's Boeing 747 G-AWNB undertook crew training at the airport. With Lloyd's growing fleet of Boeing 707s and Channel's Tridents and Comets, Stansted was experiencing a more modern (and noisier) variety of aerial visitors.

Making the news headlines was becoming a regular event for Stansted. In 1972 there were two incidents. On 5 January an Aztec light aircraft crashed on its approach to runway 23, killing three people, while September saw the arrival of the first refugees from Uganda, fleeing from the tyranny of President Idi Amin. Donaldson, British Caledonian and BOAC carried the grateful passengers to safety in England.

FORTUNES DESCEND AGAIN

The two resident airlines Lloyd and Channel began to falter, victims of the apparent curse of the airport, and suffered crippling financial problems just when Stansted's situation looked at its most positive. The Middle East oil crisis loomed large over the whole aviation industry and Lloyd's American routes had proved so costly to run that the receivers had to be called in. Channel, meanwhile, were forced to cut back all operations for a short period until they ceased flying altogether in February 1972. This was a major blow to Stansted's fluctuating fortunes and consequently Aviation Traders, who had large contracts to service the Lloyd fleet, had to cut back half of its staff. To compound the hardship, several American charter carriers such as Universal Airlines and American Flyers also either folded or curtailed their business dramatically in this year; indeed, of the transatlantic operators only Saturn remained at Stansted.

Despite an increase of European traffic from the likes of JAT, TAP, Air Portugal and the returned Braathens in 1972, Stansted seemed to be struggling once again. Passenger figures fell back in the ensuing two years from 493,000 in 1971 to 176,000 in 1973, and the previous two years of healthy growth made this downturn all the more agonizing.

Long-term prospects seemed even gloomier when it was proposed that London's third airport was to be an offshore development on reclaimed land at Maplin Sands. Despite this far-fetched and wholly impractical plan, Parliament even began to discuss the relocation of Stansted's workforce to the new airport upon its suggested opening in 1980. At this point, and not for the first time, it seemed that Stansted was surplus to requirements and heading for closure. But just when things seemed at their worst, BAA Chairman Nigel Foullks, in his annual report, foresaw that the urgent need for a third airport for London could mean that Stansted would sneak in through the back door. If there was any delay in getting a new airport up and running it would not be long before Gatwick and Heathrow reached breaking point and Stansted was in a position to capitalize – as those at BAA knew only too well, plans like Maplin Sands often remained no more than plans!

NEW HOPE AND LAKER RETURNS!

Freddie Laker's long and eventful history with Stansted looked set to continue when he launched the Laker Airways' Skytrain – a planned budget service to New York using McDonnell-Douglas DC-10s. But by 1974, despite government approval, the Skytrain service had not got off the ground because the American authorities had vetoed Laker's plans to fly this route. This enabled major companies such as British Airways and Pan Am to retain their monopoly of the Atlantic skies, and it was not until 1977 that Skytrain's inaugural service finally took off – rather disappointingly from Gatwick, not Stansted. Then Laker Airways' competitors became a new and fiercer opposition to his pioneering venture.

The oil crisis that had virtually destroyed the growth enjoyed in the first two years of the decade actually saved the airport in July 1974. As a result of the industry-wide decrease in air traffic, forecasts of future traffic were now more conservatively estimated. This made Maplin Sands look like a too costly and unnecessary investment by the government. Stansted could cope with growth to three million passengers with its existing facilities and the local council took a more lenient stance towards this more reasonable expansion plan. As predicted by the Chairman of BAA only a year before, Stansted was in a perfect position to take its place as London's third airport after all.

HIJACK!

Stansted's designation as London's official terminus for hijacked aircraft was first tested when the airport witnessed a major incident in 1975. A BAC 1-11 on a flight between Manchester and Heathrow was hijacked by an Islamic terrorist, Saaed Madjd, who took a steward hostage and demanded to be taken to Paris. Stansted was quickly 'disguised' as Orly Airport in Paris and the aircraft duly landed; the police arrested the hijacker without the need for the SAS troops who had arrived to deal with the situation. The only alleged injury occurred when a police dog bit a crew member's posterior.

Other more scheduled arrivals meant that in 1975 Stansted's passenger numbers climbed again to 238,000 with over one-fifth of them being carried by Fordair. This growth was not sustained, and in 1976 figures declined again, with Stansted's regular services down to only thirty-two a week. Without a consistent scheduled base the airport's passenger growth would always be precarious.

In 1977 another generation of aircraft visited Stansted commercially for the first time. A South African Airways 747, diverted from Heathrow, arrived in January as the first passenger-laden 'Jumbo' to use the airport; another newcomer, an Airbus A300 of TEA, followed it two months later. Jet-powered traffic was now the norm, with Boeing 707s and 737s and Douglas DC-8s the most regular sights. In 1978 El Al, the Israeli national airline, began their long association with the airport, using it for charters to Tel Aviv. BAA's security was stepped up to counter the terrorist threat to El Al jets.

On 23 August 1978 Stansted went jumbo crazy, when another baggage handling dispute diverted thirteen Heathrow-bound aircraft to Essex. Among them were no fewer than eight Boeing 747s, adding over five thousand passengers to the regular daily intake. Nothing could have highlighted more vividly the fact that Stansted was operating well below its potential capacity and that it was ready to expand as soon as the government gave the green light.

MERGING TOWARDS THE EIGHTIES

The year 1979 saw a development that was to affect Stansted's daily movements for many years. Air Anglia had begun flying domestic services from Stansted soon after merging with British Island Airways, Air Wales and Air West to form the fledgling carrier Air UK. The initial fleet consisted of twenty Handley Page Heralds, ten Fokker Friendships, and a number of BAC 1-11s and Bandeirantes. Air UK was to be a major operator throughout the next two decades and beyond, despite its change of ownership in the late 1990s.

The creation of another Stansted regular occurred in the same year when TAC Heavylift Cargo was formed. An associate company of Transmeridian, latterly known as British Cargo Airlines, Heavylift initially used three giant Short Belfast transports bought from the RAF. But just as Heavylift Cargo began to get their operation running, their sister company British Cargo Airlines ceased operating and put their aircraft into storage, leaving Heavylift as the main freight specialist at the airport. Both Air UK and Heavylift would be an integral part of the expanding Stansted.

NEW DECADE – NEW PLANS

In 1980 BAA finally submitted a plan to expand and develop the existing facilities at the airport to cater for a maximum of fifteen million passengers. The plan claimed that a major development would no longer be needed to support the airport; it required only a terminal that could cope with fifty aircraft, with parking space for 4,000 cars, along with other amenities such as a hotel. Despite this revised and more reasonable proposal, local residents were still aggrieved – they were supported this time by British Airways, who wanted to increase Heathrow's monopoly and importance by adding a fifth terminal. Options such as Maplin Sands and the possible upgrading of an ex-RAF base were also still under consideration, despite Stansted's obvious advantages.

Meanwhile, flying movements increased when Sterling moved its Scandinavian services from Luton to Stansted. They added five departures a week to the airport's roster, using Boeing 727s or Aerospatiale Caravelles. In addition, Stansted continued to provide facilities for aircraft diverted from Heathrow; one interesting arrival was a wartime Consolidated B-24 Liberator bomber, passing through from India to its new home in America. By the early 1980s changes were afoot in the non-commercial units resident at the airport. First, the Civil Aviation Authority's Flying Unit swapped their De Havilland Doves for the newer Avro 748s. More sentimentally, the Fire Training School left for a new home at Teesside Airport. Air UK began a service to Amsterdam, significant because it was the only scheduled European route from the airport, and thus began the airline's association with Holland and eventually its national carrier, KLM. Air UK used Schiphol as one of its most profitable routes for many years.

Early in 1982 another hijack was played out on Stansted's apron. In February an Air Tanzania Boeing 737 was diverted to Stansted by its captors. It sat on the tarmac for over twenty-four hours until the siege was brought to a peaceful resolution. Stansted reverted briefly to a military role in 1982 when Heavylift was contracted by the Ministry of Defence to fly out equipment to the Ascension Islands to help the Task Force during the Falklands campaign. That same year had also seen an increase in IT charters for the likes of Britannia, JAT to Yugoslavia and Wardair's transatlantic service to Canada, and Stansted's income was up by 21 per cent with passenger throughput back up to 300,000. New type arrivals included the first Illyushin IL-76, brought in by Iraqi Airways, but later a common sight on former Eastern bloc cargo routes.

One of the most spectacular events ever to grace Stansted was the arrival and static display of the NASA Space Shuttle *Enterprise* in June 1983. Brought to Britain on the back of its Boeing 747 transporter in a 'once in a lifetime' tour, the crowds who queued down the M11 motorway to see the shuttle reputedly numbered over a quarter of a million. Once again, the huge runway made the airport the obvious choice as the venue for the giant Shuttle's arrival. Also visiting that year was the Goodyear 'blimp', over from America via Calais.

By now Air UK was operating scheduled services to Paris, Brussels and Amsterdam, and in 1983 it announced its intention to make Stansted its major operations hub. This meant that there would be at least eight daily departures by one Air UK service. Along with Jersey European, Air UK made the airport a realistic business commuter proposition for the first time. IT charters simultaneously rose by a further 52 per cent in 1983, with a total of over half a million passengers in 1984/5. The uplift in movements was matched by an upgrade of facilities; the runway was one of the first in Europe to have a visual approach slope guidance system.

The drama continued on Stansted's aprons in June 1984 when a former Nigerian minister, Umaru Dikko, was found drugged and kidnapped in a crate at the airport. Mr Dikko, an alleged fraudster, was wanted back in Lagos to face charges and a mercenary team was hired to return him. The plot failed when police swooped to his rescue as he lay unconscious and crated aboard a Nigeria Airways Boeing 707 cargo jet.

THE WHITE PAPER BECOMES A BLUEPRINT

On 5 June 1985, exactly forty-one years and a day after the Marauders of the 344th BG left Stansted for the D-Day beaches, planning consent was finally granted for development to cope with an increase to over fifteen million passengers per year. To appease protesters' fears, the number of flights and the timetable for development would both be limited – but at last London was to have its modern third airport. Flights would number no more than 78,000 per year while further growth to fifteen million passengers would be under strict parliamentary approval. The work of the pro-development Stansted Airport Action Group had paid off and the task of building a modern practical terminal, able to expand without major upheaval, fell to the highly regarded Sir Norman Foster. Foster was famed for his design work, but this was his first airport terminal assignment – his design was radical and forward-looking, and the commercial flying industry awaited the finished article with bated breath. Work commenced in April 1986 and would last five years, by which time the airport's facilities and capacity would be changed almost beyond recognition.

During these initial years of development there were several changes. BAA became BAA plc, of which Stansted was a subsidiary. Air UK increased its scheduled destinations to twelve, including Frankfurt and Belfast. GH Stansted became an alternative handling agent to Servisair, and long-haul charters reached an all-time high. Stansted now operated services to eight Caribbean destinations, as well as Florida, New York, Hawaii, Canada, Malaysia and East Africa. The impetus of the new terminal's development seemed to have encouraged steady growth in both charter and scheduled services.

Annual passenger numbers finally broke through the one million barrier in 1988 and Stansted was on the runway and ready for take-off!

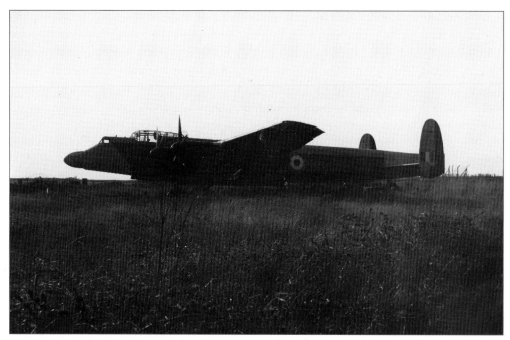

This Avro Lincoln, a former military test-bed, awaits its fate on the airfield's grassy outposts. The Lincoln was eventually used by the Fire Training School and, like so many of the training frames, was burnt out before the school departed Stansted. There was a happy postscript to this, however! The tail-wheel of the Lincoln was salvaged from the charred remains in perfect condition and was subsequently passed on to the grateful RAF for use on the Battle of Britain Memorial Flight's Avro Lancaster. (*Peter Pallet Collection*)

Heavy jets were steadily increasing the frequency of their operations to Stansted and by 1970 their proliferation in the world's skies was widespread. Here, three Boeing 707s, operated by JAT, Lloyd International and British Midland, line up on the rain-soaked apron in 1971. On the right is a Dan-Air BAC 1-11. (*Peter Pallet Collection*)

Martinair Douglas DC-6s were seen at Stansted in 1970 when a dockers' strike at British ports meant that the airport was promoted as an important cargo route. (*Peter Pallet Collection*)

A Vickers Vanguard on final approach during the 1970s. This type was used by BEA for training flights at the still relatively quiet airport. (*Peter Pallet Collection*)

Stansted's cargo has always been diverse . . . and some moved faster than others! Above, a McLaren team racing car heads off to Kuala Lumpur for a race in 1970 aboard a Lloyd International Boeing 707 after a careful loading procedure. The less speedy passenger on the left obviously does not trust the in-flight catering, catching a quick meal before boarding Transmeridian G-ATZI. This is one of the last Canadair CL-44s still in operation: working in Liberia for Translloyd Cargo, it is now approaching its fortieth birthday. (*BAA Stansted*)

American Flyers operated Inclusive Tour (IT) charters from Stansted using Douglas DC-8s. This one, pictured in summer 1971, is receiving full attention from the Servisair ground staff while the 'Avgas' tanks in the wing are topped up. Servisair was appointed as the official handling agent by BAA in 1968 and has maintained this responsibility to date. (*BAA Stansted*)

This is a sight that aviation enthusiasts would flock to see now: a 'Connie' at Stansted. Indian diplomatic and military flights were regularly undertaken by Lockheed Constellations to the airport – indeed, they were ordered to Stansted after officials at Heathrow and RAF Northolt complained that the four piston engines leaked too much oil on to the concrete! (*Peter Pallet Collection*)

Since the Berlin Airlift in 1948 humanitarian efforts have always made use of Stansted. In 1972 flights were chartered to Uganda when President Idi Amin allowed the departure of political refugees to England; here, some of the first arrive on board a BOAC Boeing 707. In total eighteen thousand refugees arrived at Stansted to start new lives in Britain. (*BAA Stansted*)

Monarch Bristol Britannia G-ANCE revs up on the runway in 1973. This aircraft had been stored at Stansted for four years prior to its purchase by Monarch. Indeed its history at the airport stretches back to the late 1950s when it operated Air Charter's long-haul services out of Stansted. The airline's destinations included Australia, America, the Middle East and Canada, until Air Charter was merged into British United Airways in 1960. (*BAA Stansted*)

Twenty years after the USAF extended Stansted's runway, a passenger aircraft worthy of such facilities arrived. On 10 January 1977 South African Airways Boeing 747-244B was the first passenger-laden 'Jumbo' to arrive at Stansted. This was clearly a turning point in the airport's history, even though it was the result of a baggage-handling problem at Heathrow. (*BAA Stansted*)

SAA's ZS-SAN Lebombo is pictured at rest on the south apron at Stansted. This 747 was delivered to SAA's fleet in October 1971 and is still in service with the airline at the time of writing. In the background, another two SAA Boeing 707s can be seen; the nearest one is ZS-SAA Johannesburg. After various leases, including a brief stint with British Midland, this venerable workhorse was finally retired in 1984. (*BAA Stansted*)

A scene from Stansted – or somewhere in Norway? This extraordinary array of aircraft, all operated by Scandinavian airlines, includes a Braathens-Safe Boeing 737 and a Stirling Caravelle, split by two SAS DC-9s. Scandinavian routes were notable for their considerable increase in 1977, helping to lift Stansted's annual passenger figures over 300,000. (*BAA Stansted*)

An aerial view across the southern area of Stansted during the 1970s, with an array of propliners on the tarmac stands. Note the many wartime buildings, hangars and huts, formerly of the 2nd TAD, still standing. On the far side of the runway a Boeing 747 Jumbo sits parked with a rather leafy backdrop! (*BAA Stansted*)

The first El Al charter arrived at Stansted in April 1978. The Israeli national airline subsequently commenced weekly charters to Ben Gurion Airport, Tel Aviv, with their Boeing 707s. After initial high loads, the service was run with 747s for some years. (*BAA Stansted*)

A extraordinarily large amount of machinery seems to be involved in loading this Seaboard World Boeing 747 at Stansted in the late 1970s. The American cargo airline operated several of these aircraft before a merger with Flying Tigers saw their aircraft transferred into the latter's livery. (*BAA Stansted*)

Although its home base was at nearby Luton Airport, Britannia Airways (known as Euravia until the purchase of a fleet of Bristol Britannias) operated its Boeing 737-200s from Stansted on IT charters to European holiday destinations such as Palma from the late 1970s. Here G-AVRN taxies north. (*BAA Stansted*)

On the tarmac at Stansted is Fokker F-28 SE-DGE *Erik Viking* of the Swedish carrier Linjeflyg, prior to that airline's merger with SAS in 1993. Linjeflyg operated daily flights from Stansted during the late 1970s, and SAS continues to operate from the airport to this day. (*BAA Stansted*)

Two Boeing 747s, both diverted from Heathrow, at rest on the apron at Stansted. Aircraft from the now defunct Pan American, KLM and South African Airlines await return to their regular routes. (*BAA Stansted*)

Although a vast improvement on the Nissen huts of the postwar airport, the 1969-built terminal looks modest in the light of the latest offering for passengers at Stansted. However, the importance of this terminal was that it upgraded Stansted's facilities in line with those of Heathrow and Gatwick, if on a smaller scale. This new-found status was highlighted by the airport's ability to deal with thirty-five diverted Heathrow-bound airliners in one day in December 1969. (*BAA Stansted*)

One of Air Express International's two Canadair CL-44s, which operated for the American cargo airline from Stansted between 1980 and 1985. N121AE was named *City of Stamford* while its sister plane was called *Dixie*. Only thirty-nine examples of the accident-prone CL-44s were used for civil purposes, the original design being a Canadian development of the Bristol Britannia. (*BAA Stansted*)

When the Olympics were held in Moscow in 1980 Aeroflot advertised their involvement via their fleet's livery. Here a suitably liveried Tupolev TU-154 is pictured at Stansted. The TU-154, a medium-range three-engined airliner, was first delivered to Aeroflot in 1972 and over seven hundred A and B variants were made. Aeroflot today continues to operate cargo services from Stansted using DC-10-30s. (*BAA Stansted*)

Concorde's first visit to Stansted was a special charter service in 1980. The British Airways 747 in the background was diverted from its scheduled destination of Heathrow owing to bad weather conditions. It was clearly common during this period for aircraft to be diverted to Stansted either because of the weather or because of occasional industrial disputes. (*BAA Stansted*)

The BAe 146 (later renamed the Avro RJ) made its public debut at Stansted on 13 October 1981. The much vaunted 'whisper jet' was registered G-SSSH, suggesting that even this prototype was quieter than normal. The aircraft, the first of many, first flew on 3 September and was delivered to Dan-Air in May 1983. The series is still in production. (*Peter Pallet Collection*)

Some passengers really are treated like cattle. . . . A herd of cows await transfer from their makeshift pens on to an Air France Boeing 747F under the watchful eye of the farmers. Once they are successfully rounded up on to the plane, the jumbo taxies out for departure. Air France still operates freight services from the airport, using its fleet of 747s. (*BAA Stansted*)

A DC-9 of Yugoslavian JAT, who commenced weekly services to Pula from Stansted in 1982, sits parked next to Aviogenex Boeing 737 on the north apron. (*Peter Pallet Collection*)

This unlikely piece of baggage passed through the airport in July 1982. Young Mark Cayley wrote to the BBC's *Jim'll Fix It* programme, hoping to fulfil his ambition of being a suitcase for a day! (*BAA Stansted*)

Sunrise and sunset! Sunrise Airlines launched its Stansted-based services to Orlando in July 1982 with a Boeing 707 and some media attention. However, the planned weekly operation was halted on only its second proposed journey owing to poor ticket sales – hence Sunrise flew only one return flight! The 707 still bears the Sabena tail livery – the airline that Sunrise had leased the aircraft from. It was bought by NATO in 1988. (*BAA Stansted*)

Nocturnal activity at Stansted as a Dan-Air BAC 1-11 in the foreground receives attention from the ground staff in 1982. This aircraft, then registered G-BJYL, is still in use, having been bought by Oriental Airlines in 1994. In the background a pair of Fokker F27 Friendships, one belonging to Dan-Air and the other to Air UK, are at rest on the floodlit northern apron. (*BAA Stansted*)

A near-disastrous incident occurred on 5 September 1982 when this Flying Tigers DC-8, N786FT, was struck by another DC-8, RP-C830, operated by Intercontinental Airlines of Nigeria, which was taking off in very poor visibility. The Flying Tigers freighter, which was preparing to load in the cargo area, received damage to its tailplane, while the Nigerian airliner, with fifty-seven passengers on board, suffered damage to its wing and flaps. It continued to Manchester for an emergency landing where it was impounded for non-payment of airport fees; adding insult to injury, many of the startled passengers were arrested for drug offences and passport irregularities at Manchester! RP-C830's association with Stansted did not end there, as the DC-8 was eventually broken up at the airfield in 1984. (*BAA Stansted*)

A momentous day at Stansted: on 5 June 1983 the NASA Space Shuttle *Enterprise* arrived at the airport as part of its European Tour. *Enterprise* was carried 'piggy-back' across the Atlantic by a specially modified Boeing 747-100. The Jumbo required customized stabilizers on its tail in order to fly safely and the sight of it cruising over the Essex countryside was indeed a unique one! As you can see from the aerial photograph, the Shuttle was a huge attraction and it is estimated that over a quarter of a million spectators came to view it during its two-day stay in England – causing major delays on the M11 motorway! (*BAA Stansted*)

In honour of the Space Shuttle's visit to Stansted, Air UK named one of its Stansted-based fleet of Short 330-200s *Enterprise*. The huge hulk of the Shuttle and its Jumbo can just be seen parked in the distance. The Short aircraft, G-BKDN, only served with Air UK for nine months of its thirteen-year life-span, eventually being broken up in 1995. With its scheduled movements growing, Air UK was becoming ever more important to the airport at this time. (*BAA Stansted*)

Another unusual visitor arrived in July 1983 when the Goodyear 'blimp' flew in from America. Naturally this aroused special interest as well as requiring special handling by the airport staff. Here the airship arrives while the airport operations team waits below. (*BAA Stansted*)

A pilot's view of the approach to runway 050 at Stansted in 1984, over the Bishop's Stortford–Takely road. Note the T2 hangar on the right-hand side of the runway, which was removed during the sweeping changes made to the airport later in the decade. (*Peter Pallet Collection*)

Little and large at Stansted! A Transamerica Airlines Boeing 747-200 waits behind Air UK's Short 330-200 on the apron in late 1984. The Jumbo is over 230ft in length, compared to the Short's 58ft. This particular 747 was one of several charters flying between the USA and Stansted which helped to account for over 40,000 transatlantic passengers in the 1984/5 period – a tenfold increase on the previous year. This demonstrated the increasing need for another major terminus for London-bound air passengers. (*BAA Stansted*)

Former Stansted Operations Officer Reg Robinson pictured in 1984 outside a derelict wartime building. This was the gun turret overhaul centre used by the mechanics of the USAAF in 1944. The bullets were found in a nearby ditch – where they were thrown at about the same time. Sadly, this historic building has disappeared from the airport as a result of the development in the late 1980s; it used to stand on the south side of the airfield, close to the site of today's Diamond hangar. (*Peter Pallet Collection*)

The old control tower at Stansted, pictured in the mid-1980s. This is clearly an extension of the standard USAAF control tower built at Stansted during the war. The original centre portion of this building was upgraded and extended through the years, until its inevitable replacement as part of the recent modernization of the airport. (*Peter Pallet Collection*)

This is a sight not seen at a British airport in some time! An Iraqi Airways Ilyushin IL-76 sits on one of the old runways, waiting for its cargo to be unloaded. Iraqi Airways was the first airline to use this aircraft at Stansted, in September 1982. (*BAA Stansted*)

Given the airfield's proximity to the Dagenham factory and Brentwood headquarters, the Ford Motor Company based its corporate air fleet at Stansted for many years, taking over one of the old wartime T2 hangars in 1967. Here, pictured in October 1985, a BAC 1-11 (G-BFMC), a Grumman G-159 Gulfstream 1 (G-BRAL) and a G-1159 Gulfstream 2 (N328K) sit outside the Ford Air hangar. (*Tony Rogers*)

Concorde made an occasional appearance throughout the decade thanks to diversions and special charters, as well as promotional flights and Stansted 'staff outings'. Concorde never fails to draw the crowds, and over five thousand people came to see her in 1985 when this photograph was taken. (*BAA Stansted*)

American Trans-Air (ATA) Lockheed L-1011 Tri-Star, registered N709DA, pictured on the concrete at Stansted in the summer of 1985. ATA flew from Stansted to North America during the 1980s and still operates a large fleet from its Indiana base, although no longer to the UK. The American heavy jet is somewhat overshadowed by the sight of Concorde taking off after one of her infrequent visits to Essex. (*BAA Stansted*)

The US charter airline Eagle Air was another of the growing number of such airlines using Stansted during the mid-1980s to capitalize on the American tourists' demand for holidays in Britain. This DC-8 is pictured on the tarmac in 1985. Note the Aviation Traders' crew giving the airliner its necessary attention. (*BAA Stansted*)

Memphis-based Federal Express was one of the first regular transatlantic users of Stansted's freight capabilities and it continues to have a large presence even now. Their five-nights-a-week service began with the Boeing 727-200 (pictured) in 1985, but this was quickly replaced by Fedex's McDonnell Douglas DC-10 fleet. The service has since progressed to MD-11s. (*BAA Stansted*)

In 1986 Sir Norman Foster unveiled his vision for Stansted's future. He described the new terminal as majoring on 'calm, clarity and convenience', with passengers being able to go from the entrance, through the check-in desks, customs and gates in an easy 'straight line progress' from the front to the back of the building. The terminal was built to accommodate eight million passengers per annum in an airy, quiet and spacious environment. (*BAA Stansted*)

A Cargolux Douglas DC-8 lifts from the tarmac. This freighter airline now has a fleet of Boeing 747Fs, which can still be seen at Stansted. (*BAA Stansted*)

A pair of Jumbos fill the concrete in June 1986. A 747 of Canadian Wardair was regularly used for charter services across the Atlantic during this period, although its partner was paying Stansted a more unusual visit: Northwest Orient's brand new N637US arrived at the airport in order to take part in a formation flight with a DC-3 at nearby North Weald's annual airshow. (*BAA Stansted*)

Alan Haslehurst, MP for Stansted (left), and Michael Spicer, then minister for aviation, congratulate each other on the official commencement of the airport's £290 million upgrade, April 1986. (*BAA Stansted*)

SU-DAE of the Egyptian airline Zarkani Aviation Service has its engines stripped for service outside the old Aviation Traders hangar in September 1987. Luxor went on to have an interesting life: in 1996 she was purchased by the United States Air Force after conversion to a military E-8C – twenty-eight years after her maiden flight. (*Tony Rogers*)

Echoes of Stansted's past could be heard in the spring of 1987 when there was a temporary renaissance for piston-engined aircraft at the airport. As a publicity stunt to mark the grand announcement of the privatization of Rolls-Royce, the company flew in some of the more illustrious aircraft its engines had powered, such as the Avro Lancaster, Hawker Hurricane and de Havilland Mosquito. These Merlin-engined planes provided an interesting contrast to the giant Rolls-Royce-powered jets of the modern era. (*BAA Stansted*)

A Flying Tigers' Boeing 747-200 freighter pictured at Stansted's cargo loading area, 13 April 1987. The cargo being loaded was to be delivered to Karachi on behalf of the British Livestock Agency. N807FT came to an untimely and tragic end less than two years later when it crashed into a mountain on approach to Kuala Lumpur airport in Malaysia. (*BAA Stansted*)

In the 1960s all new Handley Page Heralds built at Radlett were test-flown to Stansted to check the Instrument Landing Systems (ILS) before delivery. Here a veteran Herald of South East Air sits parked on the old cargo area apron on the airport's north side in 1987. South East Air used G-CEAS for six months before returning it to Channel Express Air Services. Within six years Channel Express had retired from service all the world's working Heralds. (*Tony Rogers*)

The Yugoslavian government used Stansted in the late 1980s for transport flights to Sarajevo. Here Antonov An-12B YU-AIC departs in April 1987; its sister ship YU-AID followed minutes later. (*Tony Rogers*)

A Heavylift Boeing 707 prepares to receive its cargo via the specially designed loading mechanism. Established in 1980 as a sister company of long-time Stansted resident Transmeridian, Heavylift has expanded rapidly, filling a niche by specializing in carrying cargo for a variety of industry sectors including aerospace, automotive and even famine relief. Using Stansted as its operational base, Heavylift's fleet has been a regular sight at the airport over the last two decades. (*BAA Stansted*)

Aer Turas Teoranta Douglas DC-8-63CF EI-BNA *City of Dublin* receives its cargo of racehorses on the former cargo apron on the northern side of Stansted before departing runway 23 (below) in August 1987. This Irish airline currently operates two DC-8s and a Lockheed Tristar from its Dublin base. Note the old control tower at the side of the runway as the plane climbs off the tarmac. (*Tony Rogers*)

In April 1987 Boeing 747-287 G-VIRG undertook Virgin Atlantic's crew training at Stansted. *Maiden Voyager*, seen here above runway 23, completed a number of 'touch and go' circuits. It would be unimaginable for the airport to accommodate such a service today owing to the increased traffic at Stansted. (*Tony Rogers*)

CHAPTER FIVE

LONDON STANSTED – MILLENNIUM GATEWAY

By 1989 the new facilities at Stansted were taking shape and beginning to enter service. The new cargo sheds opened for use after a £4.5 million construction, which now gave the airport eight stands for freighter aircraft up to the size of a Boeing 747. The Diamond hangar – a £20m facility for servicing airliners – won Stansted the first of several construction and architecture awards when it opened in 1989 revealing its 'double triangle' shape, which maximized the area for servicing aircraft. For passengers, the Hilton Hotel was constructed north of the runway.

The introduction of the Irish budget airline Ryanair was to prove a major boost to future scheduled traffic. They began Stansted operations with a service to Knock using their ageing BAC 1-11s. Their presence grew rather rapidly though and a Dublin route was soon added. The anti-monopoly laws in Ireland meant that Aer Lingus could not compete against Ryanair on these routes for three years, allowing the fledgling carrier to gain a valuable foothold in the UK market that it was to use to good effect, becoming more and more important to the airport.

With the fall of the 'Iron Curtain' and the prospect of new facilities for passengers just around the corner, new routes and new operators began to appear on Stansted's departure boards. By August 1990 there were 167 scheduled flights to seventeen destinations each week and airlines such as Aeroflot quickly capitalized on new opportunities, using the new cargo sheds to expand its usage of Stansted as well as introduce the giant Antonov An. 124 to the airport.

In 1990, however, economic depression and the cloud of the Gulf War affected much of the industry, with demand for holiday flights cut back thanks to the increased fear of terrorist attacks on both sides of the Atlantic. This hit Stansted's charter trade dramatically, with IT operators cutting back their services or retreating to established hubs at Luton and Gatwick. However, by this time a sufficiently large scheduled flight base had been built up at Stansted, which offset the long-term damage to business, and passenger numbers did not decrease below a million for 1990/1. The development was in its final stages when the terminal was opened by HM the Queen in March 1991 and it entered into commercial use only days after the royal visit. Fittingly, an Air UK flight to Glasgow was the first departure from Sir Norman Foster's wonderful creation.

By May 1991 Stansted had recovered from its economic downturn in double-quick time and scheduled footfall had been enlarged by 60 per cent on the previous year. This was primarily thanks to the ongoing growth of Ryanair and Air UK who were both expanding their businesses at Stansted. Jersey European was also becoming increasingly active on its short-haul routes. In 1991 Stansted saw over 1.6 million travellers pass through its new terminal (representing a massive 46 per cent growth on 1990) and charter flights also began to gradually return over the next few years.

New buildings and facilities were rapidly turning Stansted into a modern airport at the cutting edge of design and layout. The new ILS landing system allowed more aircraft to land more safely, and a new fire station was built adjacent to the cargo sheds and the runway. Infrastructure including car parks, a railway station and a staff training centre were also added. Plaudits were inevitable. BAA, along with Foster and Partners, had designed a terminal for the twenty-first century and at first glance the whole development showed foresight and aesthetic creativity unlike any airport seen previously in Europe. Decorations such as the prestigious Mies van de Rohe Pavilion Award and the British Construction Industry Supreme Award were high praise for Foster's work and the landscaping of the 'new' Stansted. As befitted an airport with such superb facilities, business continued to grow to cope with the added demand on London's skies. By the end of 1991 nearly 1.7 million passengers had passed through Stansted, with the growth in cargo also noticeable – by May 1992 freight volumes had increased by 30 per cent on the previous year thanks largely to Federal Express, UPS, Aeroflot and Heavylift.

This expansion continued steadily during the latter half of 1990s. Ryanair, with its cut-price fares to Ireland and beyond, soon brought over half a million passengers through Stansted each year, with Air UK not far behind that figure. Many new airlines arrived to ply their trade at one of the most advanced airports in the world. The ever-increasing routes undertaken by major scheduled carriers such as Lufthansa, KLM, Aer Lingus, Air France and El Al ensured that over half of Stansted's users were and still are national 'flag carriers' – a mark of the airport's enhanced status.

Stansted was growing at a dramatic rate, even though it fell behind the initial prediction that eight million people would be using the airport by 1995; however, in that year there were over eight hundred scheduled flights at the airport each week (as opposed to eight just over a decade before). Flight movements also began to exceed the initial 70,000-odd planned per year and were up to over 100,000 by the end of 1998, although the reintroduction of transatlantic and high-loading long-haul business proved elusive.

Year (Jan–Dec)	Passenger figures (in millions)
1994	3.26
1995	3.89
1996	4.81
1997	5.37
1998	6.83

(Figures courtesy of BAA plc)

ALL SYSTEMS GO

Stansted approached the new millennium busier than ever and is acknowledged by airlines and public alike as a great place to fly from. Once again there were changes and new arrivals as the big players noticed Stansted's potential and growing importance as they jostled for position. In February 1998 KLM took its relationship with Air UK one step further. Having acquired the entire airline in 1997, it created a new brand, KLM uk, to replace the existing Air UK operations and fleet liveries. Not only was this part of KLM's brand extension, it was also a means for the company to continue to feed its main Schipol hub, only 45 minutes' flying time from Stansted. It was the end of an era, however, as Air UK had been so fundamental to the foundation of scheduled services at Stansted over the previous two decades.

British Airways reacted quickly to the growth in 'budget' airlines in northern Europe undercutting its traditional routes. The BA-owned Go Fly was launched amid a fanfare of publicity in May 1998 using Stansted as its base. Barbara Cassani, chief executive of Go Fly, said 'I wanted an airport that sent out the same message about air travel that we were trying to convey . . . simple to use, clean, modern and efficient.' Within eighteen months Go Fly had over a dozen regular routes and a growing fleet of brand new Boeing 737s operating almost hourly out of London Stansted. The formation of Go Fly and its Luton-based rival EasyJet meant customers increasingly used telephone and internet booking to great effect, the airlines even dispensing with the traditional ticket and boarding cards. This streamlined the way airlines interact with their customers and made flying from a modern airport like Stansted, where efficiency is now built into the whole philosophy of both airline and airport, extremely simple. Even KLM decided to adopt this strategy when in October 1999 it announced plans to create a new brand, Buzz, which was to offer similar budget-priced flights from Stansted to the continent, in effect taking over part of the role filled by KLM uk.

The highly profitable Ryanair continued to add to its routes and update its fleet of 737s, and by 1999 was Stansted's largest operator with over 600 flights a week and around 30 per cent of the airport's traffic. Ryanair, KLM uk, Aer Lingus, Go Fly and the other twenty or so scheduled carriers all contributed to make Stansted Britain's fourth largest airport with an amazing 8.5 million passengers between September 1998 and August 1999. With 83 per cent of passengers flying one of the sixty-nine scheduled routes, the airport's growth at last had a secure base. Indeed August 1999 alone saw over a million passengers pass through Stansted as the daily movements at the airport averaged over 450, making it one of Europe's fastest growing airports.

Stansted has been officially titled London's 'Millennium Gateway' as a mark of pride in the achievements of the past decade. The quality of airport design now has a new benchmark. Stansted has received much praise for its consumer-friendly environment and spectacular and innovative design, as well as its rapid growth. Stansted's development embodies many unique or influential facets.

THE TERMINAL

The spacious and airy design of high, connected canopied roofing gives Stansted a wholly unique feel, very different to the almost claustrophobic atmosphere found in many of Europe's ageing airports. Sir Norman Foster's design provides passengers with the feeling of space, light and ease of movement. The whole philosophy is that passengers make 'straight line' progress on a single floor from front to back of the terminal, avoiding stairs, lifts and non-linear passage, reaching the aircraft within about 150 metres.

The 32,000 square metre construction has an all-glass outer shell and canopied roofs which allow natural light to illuminate the terminal and its wide concourses. The terminal has two satellites, set back from the main building, where passengers enter or leave their aircraft. The satellites and the terminal are connected by a 'people mover' train system. This separation allows the main terminal to be used as a transit area only, and also allows for simple expansion in future years by extension at either side.

The terminal was initially designed for eight million passengers per year but has exceeded that capacity already, coping with an average of over two thousand passengers per hour. Stansted has a good selection of shops and services for passengers, although the loss of duty free concessions in 1999 on European Union flights hit the airport's revenue hard – the predicted loss totalling around £13m per year. The new Millennium Lounge affords customers all the comforts of a first-class lounge for a small fee (£10 in 1999), providing a calm haven even for those flying on Stansted's regular 'budget' operators.

The satellites have over two dozen gates with the latest 'jetways' allowing passengers to board the aircraft in full comfort. Satellite One is for international flights and has seating for nearly two thousand; Satellite Two is used mainly for domestic purposes, although it was opened to international passengers in 1998 to meet the growing demand. It can now cope with an extra two million international travellers each year.

A railway station is incorporated into the terminal below the front entrance, allowing quick access to and from London's Liverpool Street station on the 'Stansted Express'.

THE CARGO TERMINAL

In May 1989 the new cargo terminal opened. Located adjacent to the main passenger terminal and new ATC control tower, Stansted's cargo facilities have dramatically improved, immediately increasing the turnover of freight business the airport enjoyed. By 1998 the freight total passing through the 'World Cargo Centre' was up to 180,000 tonnes – more than double the tally recorded only four years earlier and sufficient to make Stansted the third largest cargo centre in the UK.

The five transit sheds and six aircraft stands allow a fast turnover of freight, as well as a maximum capacity of over 275,000 tonnes at present. The advanced computer-based customs clearance system which Stansted shares with Heathrow and Gatwick allows each carrier to track individual cargo consignments through every stage of its journey. The changes have subsequently attracted a larger presence from the big players in the cargo market, such as Federal Express, UPS and DHL, in addition to Stansted's own Heavylift fleet.

A variety of freight passes through the facilities, from perishables to thoroughbred racehorses travelling to and from the nearby Newmarket stables. The horses are now cared for by vets, specially laid on to ensure their safe transit through Stansted's own border inspection post.

BUSINESS AVIATION

Stansted's corporate and private facilities have also enjoyed immense improvement and subsequent growth over the last decade. The former 1960s-built passenger terminal on the northern side of the runway was developed into a Business Aviation Centre to cater for private customers. The building was refurbished by Esso Petroleum and was renamed the Avitat Centre (the brand name for Esso's forty-four worldwide business aviation terminals). There are eleven aircraft stands, which can cope with various sizes of business jets, including a Boeing 747 for the wealthiest of entrepreneurs!

Although Esso owns the centre, it is available for lease by other operators. Designed for service and convenience, the Avitat Centre has 24-hour customs and immigration service, specialist catering, as well as highly equipped meeting and conference facilities. Inflite provides executive aircraft maintenance. They employ 150 people offering 24-hour support from their Executive Jet Centre, a much-developed former wartime hangar.

THE FLS DIAMOND HANGAR

FLS Aerospace provides servicing on a larger scale in the impressive Diamond hangar. Built at a cost of £20 million and opened in May 1989, the hangar not only boasts an award-winning design, but also the longest curtain rail in the world! (It's used to separate the hangar into two halves when required.) The diamond-shaped design affords over 87,000 square metres of hangar space, which is enough for two Boeing 747-400s or several smaller airliners to be accommodated at any time. FLS is one of the world's leading engineering and aviation support companies, helping numerous aircraft to stay airborne on a daily basis. Stansted is a crucial part of their UK operations.

THE ENVIRONMENT

After years of furore over the detrimental effect that Stansted's expansion would have on the environment, BAA has been careful to ensure that the airport is at the forefront of 'Green' thinking. During construction of the new terminal archaeologists were allowed to undertake one of Britain's largest ever excavation projects in tandem with the new multi-million pound development. Ten new sites of historical importance were unearthed, ranging from the Bronze Age to medieval times. The most important 'finds' were an Iron Age village and two Roman burial sites which dated back to AD 100. During development seven listed buildings were carefully dismantled and moved to safer environments in surrounding areas.

In accordance with the public inquiry recommendations, a wildlife area was created to provide safe and undisturbed habitats for plants and flowers in the airport's environs. The 10-acre site has been carefully designed and managed to fit in with the local ecological history of Stansted as well as providing an aesthetically pleasing backdrop to the airport. The wildlife area initiative has enabled the re-establishment of many insect and animal species dislocated from local farms, and as a result Stansted has an arguably more pleasant rural feel than any other airport of its size.

Noise pollution – the bane of people living near any airport – has been carefully monitored as a result of the long-held fears of local residents. Although the number of flights leaving the airport has exceeded the initial allowances, the average size of aircraft used (and therefore the subsequent noise level) has been somewhat smaller than anticipated. Regardless of this, a 24-hour automated noise recorder ensures strict adherence to CAA rules for aircraft volumes. The government has imposed a decibel limit for take-offs and landings between 11.30p.m. and 6a.m., which is intended to encourage the use of quieter aircraft in these more noise-sensitive time-slots. A central computer collates any infringements of the restrictions and penalties are levied on airlines that do so – the money raised being donated to numerous local charities and good causes as part of the 'Stansted Airport Noise Fund' initiative.

Aware of the strong opposition the airport has faced over the last three decades, BAA has clearly been at pains to give the local environment the opportunity to flourish alongside the airport rather than be overcome by it.

INTO THE FUTURE

It is possible to fly from Stansted to over sixty-five destinations on over twenty-five scheduled airlines on a weekly basis, and this number is increasing all the time, with over 95 per cent of flights now scheduled – but the £500 million investments that have been seen since 1986 will not stop there. Stansted already has planning permission to increase its capacity to fifteen million passengers and work has begun to improve the infrastructure required for this. Phase II of the expansion involves expanding the terminal at either side to accommodate a number of new check-in aisles and baggage carousels. This increase in capacity means that commercial flight movements at the airport will number over 180,000 every year by the time the expansion is completed in 2006. As a result, the number of passenger satellites will be doubled to four, new office space will be added, along with a business park, and the World Cargo Centre's area will be increased by 10,000 square metres. The expansion will cost around £200 million in total and will create 5,000 new jobs.

BAA retains its awareness of the sensitive environment, however, and maintains that not only is such an expansion consistent with the original planning permission of the 1980s but that the airport's managers 'will continue to develop measures which minimize the impact of its operations on the local community'.

Beyond this new phase, BAA forecasts that much of the growth in air traffic in future years over London will come from Stansted, coupled with the potential Terminal 5 at Heathrow; it is expected that passenger volumes will increase by 35 per cent in London's airports over the next ten years. During this period Stansted's passenger capacity will reach over twenty million with the opportunity to grow further to forty million with sufficient investment; the possibility of a second runway may well loom up again as a serious issue, and one likely to be as fiercely debated as ever.

Stansted's branding as the 'Millennium Gateway' appears apt as the airport embodies the prevailing spirit of travel – combining ease of movement, a comfortable spacious terminal with modern facilities and good value as well as expansion in an environmentally sound manner. Stansted has a history of which it can be proud, and it can look to the future with tremendous optimism.

Arriving at Stansted as part of a British sales drive is Tupolev TU-204-200. To make the Russian medium-range airliner more appealing to Western customers, the 200 series was fitted with Rolls-Royce RB211-535 engines. This airliner was launched in competition to the Boeing 757 and was first flown in 1989 before delivery to Aeroflot. (*FLS Aerospace*)

November 1988 and work is under way on the new terminal at the top of the picture, with the Diamond hangar area to the right also making good progress. This photograph illustrates the relative difference in size from the old terminal on the left of the runway. A few of the wartime 'spectacle-shaped' hardstands are still visible. (*BAA Stansted*)

This T2 hangar, which was once home to one of the squadrons of the 344th BG, was moved up the M11 to Duxford in 1989 once Stansted underwent its development. It now houses part of the Imperial War Museum's impressive display of vintage aircraft. The small doors at the top were later additions to the standard T2 hangar, in order to accommodate taller postwar aircraft. Another former 344th BG hangar is situated at North Weald. It would be fitting if they once again contained a Marauder! (*Author*)

With construction under way, Stansted's main terminal was literally dug into a hillside in order for the roof to be no higher than the local existing mature trees – therefore preventing the possibility of it becoming an eyesore. Over a million and a quarter cubic metres of earth needed to be excavated to accommodate this. (*BAA Stansted*)

Ships in the night! Owing to its location in a relatively rural area, Stansted is able to operate flights twenty-four hours a day. Although strict limits are imposed on noise levels after dark, cargo movements remain very active; indeed Stansted is one of the busiest centres of nocturnal freight movement in Britain. (*Heavylift via James Roche PR*)

The Diamond hangar on the southern side of Stansted was opened in 1989. It is home to FLS Aerospace, which conducts major and scheduled overhauls of many of Stansted's fleets from the hangar. It is an important part of FLS's maintenance and engineering division, which is responsible for the smooth running of over four hundred airliners worldwide. Here a Boeing 757 receives attention. (*FLS Aerospace*)

Her Majesty the Queen arrives at Stansted's new expanded terminal for the official opening ceremony on 15 March 1991. Commercial activity commenced only four days later with Air UK passengers the first to depart from the terminal. (*BAA Stansted*)

The largest civilian aircraft in the world, the Antonov 124, first arrived at the airport in 1991 operated by Aeroflot. You could be forgiven for thinking this a Siberian scene – the giant Russian cargo plane certainly looks at home in the snow. It was carrying 85 tonnes of heavy equipment for use on a supertanker in the United Arab Emirates. This load was barely half the maximum capacity of the aircraft. (*BAA Stansted*)

This HS.748 is currently in use by the Civil Aviation Authority's Flight Calibration Service. G-AVXI's role is to regularly visit all the major UK airports in order to check that their instrument landing systems, radar, runway lights and all the other operational necessities are in perfect working order. (*Richard Parker*)

Ensor Air was one of several airlines that sprang up in the wake of sweeping political changes in Czechoslovakia. Betraying her former CSA (the Czech national airline) ownership, this Iluyshin IL-62M (OK-BYZ) sits near the old maintenance area on the north side of the airport in 1993. (*Tony Rogers*)

A favourite haunt of the USAAF airmen, The Ash public house stands just off Stansted's perimeter at the nearby village of Burton End. The pub is still fully 'operational' today and has a display of wartime memorabilia as well as a commemorative tree planted in 1995 by a 344th pilot. (*Peter Pallet Collection*)

Two United Airlines aircraft, a Boeing 747 and 727, receive full overhauls in the Diamond hangar. The scaffold frames are tailored to suit the varying sizes of aircraft catered for in the giant hangar. (*FLS Aerospace*)

A common sight in the cargo area, this is a Turkish Cargo Boeing 727-2F2 Freighter. TC-JCD *Sinop* heads toward her parking space at the new cargo shed area. The fire station tower can be seen above the fuselage of the plane. This 727 was one of the very last of the type to be built before production ceased in 1984. (*Richard Parker*)

An early morning scene at Stansted as UPS Boeing 767 Cargo awaits departure on the airline's regular transatlantic freight services. The aircraft is painted in a colourful 'Worldwide Olympic Partner' design. (*Richard Parker*)

Passengers disembark from a BAe 146 'Whisperjet' in July 1996. The Southend-based carrier Flightline operated this service from Zurich to Stansted. The short/medium-range airliner can be configured to seat well over a hundred passengers comfortably. Note the giant new air traffic control tower rising starkly above the airport in the distance. (*Oliver Stanek*)

United Airlines Boeing 727-222 N7261U waiting to be towed back to the apron on the south side of Stansted after an engineering overhaul. Note the 727's now unorthodox passenger entrance walkway underneath the tailplane. This particular 727 was acquired as new by United in 1977 and is seen in their latest livery. (*FLS Aerospace*)

The cargo centre, which sits adjacent to the passenger satellites, is made up of five separate transit sheds and covers more than 17,000 square metres. Servisair, FedEx, TNT Express Worldwide, Ghi and the Royal Mail occupy the sheds and can handle a cumulative total of 275,000 tonnes of freight each year. There is space for six aircraft on the apron, although here a solitary TNT BAe 146 is the only occupant. Just beyond and left of the cargo area is the airport fire station with its watchtower visible. (*Author*)

MK Airlines' DC-8-55F 9G-MKF on approach to Stansted. This aircraft has enjoyed a long history since its first flight in 1965, including over two decades of service in the French Armée de l'Air. Ghanaian MK Airlines, which acquired it in 1995, are set to move their operations to Manston. (*Adam Rowden*)

A blast from the past! The Tupolev 134 is undoubtedly of 1960s origin. The prototype first flew in 1962. It was designed to carry eighty-four passengers over short/medium-range journeys. The Russian carrier Kosmos still operates over two dozen of the type; this one was photographed at Stansted in 1997. (*Richard Parker*)

SAS Fokker F-28, SE-DGH *Gunnar Viking*, sits on the hardstand in 1998, before its retirement from the airline's Stansted to Stockholm service. Douglas DC-9-41s, as well as the occasional Boeing 737-600, have now replaced the Fokkers. SAS also flies to Copenhagen using a similar range of aircraft. Linjeflyg previously operated *Gunnar Viking* before the company merged into SAS in 1993. (*Adam Rowden*)

In the early 1990s Heavylift formed an Anglo-Russian joint venture with Volga-Dnepr in order to market the giant Antonov 124-100 in the West. Heavylift now has access to seven of the freighters and they are an interesting addition to Stansted's cargo areas. (*Heavylift via James Roche PR*)

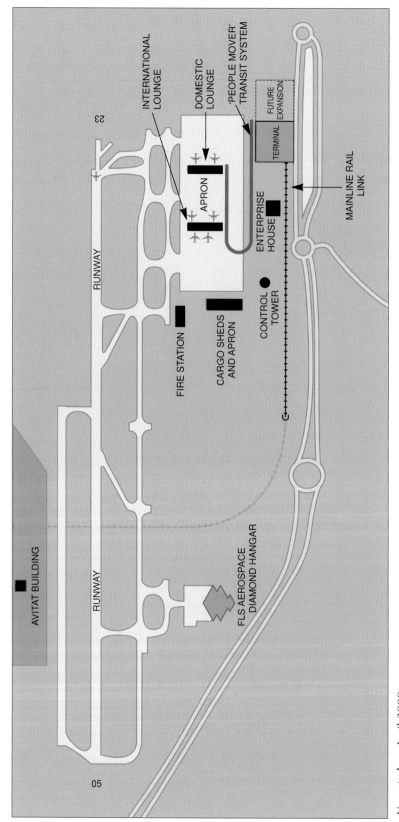

INTERNATIONAL LOUNGE

DOMESTIC LOUNGE

'PEOPLE MOVER' TRANSIT SYSTEM

FUTURE EXPANSION

TERMINAL

MAINLINE RAIL LINK

APRON

ENTERPRISE HOUSE

RUNWAY

23

CONTROL TOWER

FIRE STATION

CARGO SHEDS AND APRON

AVITAT BUILDING

RUNWAY

FLS AEROSPACE DIAMOND HANGAR

05

Airport plan, April 2000.

134

Titan Airways aircraft operate in their distinctive livery from Stansted, their operational base. The airline uses a variety of aircraft including a BAE 146-200, ATR 42-300 and, from mid-1999, a Boeing 737-300. Titan operates both as a corporate charter and freight carrier. (*Adam Rowden*)

Air Transat regularly operates summer charters from Stansted to the invariably warmer climes of Vancouver and Toronto. Here, Boeing 757 C-GTSN taxies into drizzle-bound Stansted. (*Richard Parker*)

September 1997 saw one very unusual cargo depart from Stansted. Thrust SSC was en route to its successful attempt to break the world land speed record in the Black Rock Desert in Nevada. Powered by two Spey engines, as used in RAF Phantom jets, Thrust SSC achieved a speed of 714mph. Outsize cargo specialists Heavylift-Volga Dnepr used one of their Antonov 124 freighters to transport Thrust SSC and her team across the Atlantic. Here, driver Andy Green (left) and project leader Richard Noble pose for the camera as the jet car is loaded on to the giant aircraft. (*BAA Stansted*)

Polar Air Cargo 747 N851FT *Maynard Ekedal* taxies into the cargo terminal after arriving on a dark day in August 1997. This is one of California-based Polar Air's sixteen Jumbos, many of which were previously operated by the once-mighty Pan American before being converted to freighters. N851FT once operated as part of Pan Am's global operations and was named *Clipper Witch of the Waves*. (*Richard Parker*)

Euroscot Express began 'value' flights from the south coast of England to Scotland in September 1997. BAE 1-11 G-AZMF was leased from European Aircharter for this purpose and visited Stansted for maintenance work. This airliner first flew in 1972 and had a distinguished career in the colours of British Caledonian prior to sale in 1994. (*Richard Parker*)

An unusual visitor to the airport was the 'Flying Hospital' Lockheed L-1011 TriStar owned by the humanitarian organization Operation Blessing. N787N, previously used by Pacific Southwest, Aero Peru and Worldwide Airlines, underwent a $25 million refurbishment after purchase in 1994 – and now boasts three operating theatres, two dental surgeries and a rehabilitation area. It is used for humanitarian relief in worldwide emergency situations and poverty-stricken nations. (*Richard Parker*)

February 1998 and Royal Air Maroc Boeing 747-2B *Combi* taxies towards the runway on a rare visit to Stansted. Luton-based motor manufacturer Vauxhall chartered CN-RME for a car launch in Morocco, but the Jumbo was unable to use the significantly smaller London Luton Airport, despite its geographical location adjacent to Vauxhall's HQ. (*Richard Parker*)

An Icelandair Boeing 757 in the Diamond hangar. This photograph illustrates clearly the huge proportions of the hangar. (*FLS Aerospace*)

The Diamond hangar is a specialist maintenance depot for Boeing aircraft as well as for the Airbus A300 and A320 families. The hangar can accommodate either two 747s or up to six 737s at any one time. Here a 747 is stripped down to its bare interior for maintenance and refurbishment. An airliner undergoes such a major overhaul roughly every eight years and the service can take up to a month. (*FLS Aerospace*)

The spectacular terminal designed by Sir Norman Foster. The walls are all glazed and lighting gives the terminal its unique 'airy' feel both during the day and at night. The thirty-six steel trees (six can be seen at the front of the terminal) each supports an 18 metre square roof canopy. All the passenger facilities are on a single floor level, making the passengers' journey as easy as possible. (*Richard Davies via Foster and Partners*)

C-FBUS holds the distinction of being the first Airbus A330 to operate from North America (as advertised on the fuselage!). Canadian charter operator Skyservice Airlines took delivery of the plane in May 1997, and in the same month she visited Stansted. (*Richard Parker*)

April 1998 saw a dramatic incident when a chartered Emerald Airways HS.748 developed engine problems on take-off. The pilot was forced to abort and the aircraft plunged into the soft ground at the end of the runway. The aircraft was carrying the Leeds United football team, returning from a match at West Ham to Leeds/Bradford airport. Fortunately only a few minor injuries were incurred. Assistant manager David O'Leary praised the quick reactions of pilot Captain John Haskett to the explosion in the engine. Captain Haskett was the centre of attention in the next morning's newspapers, by which time Stansted was beginning to return to normal operations. (*BAA Stansted*)

Classic Airways ceased operations in August 1998, leaving this Lockheed 1101 TriStar G-IIOI redundant only a year into its lease; it was left parked in the Golf stands at Stansted. Previously registered VR-HHK, this widebodied tri-jet aircraft served Hong Kong-based Cathay Pacific for over twenty years before they sold it on in 1996. (*Edward Warburton*)

A rare military visitor, this Kuwaiti Air Force Lockheed Hercules, registration KAF 324, appeared at Stansted in December 1998. Stansted still provides facilities for government cargo and VIP operations. This was one of several Kuwaiti Hercules visits during this period. (*Adam Rowden*)

G-UKTD sits on the apron by the new terminal satellites. This Fokker 50 was previously part of Air UK's fleet at Stansted before KLM bought a majority share in the airline and re-branded it in the colours of KLM uk in February 1998. The airline is a key player at Stansted, with services to destinations in Britain and the continent using a fleet of over forty aircraft. In the background is an Atlas Air Boeing 747F with its rear cargo doors open. This plane flies three times a week to Hong Kong via Dubai. (*Adam Rowden*)

Stansted is still a key venue for diverted flights from Britain's other international airports. Here Northwest McDonnell-Douglas DC-10 40 taxies in after being rerouted from Gatwick. Northwest is the American partner airline of KLM. (*Richard Parker*)

Falcon Air operates occasional flights from Stansted on behalf of Premair to Scandinavian destinations such as Copenhagen and Stockholm. Here, SE-DPA *Aftonfalken*, one of their fleet of three Boeing 737-300s, departs the international area of the airport. (*Richard Parker*)

Ryanair is the most frequent and one of the most important users of modern Stansted. Its fleet of Boeing 737s accounts for around 30 per cent of traffic at the airport, with nearly six hundred movements a week. Ryanair, along with Air UK, set the trend for scheduled flights from the airport. On the left is a Boeing 727 of KTHY Cyprus Turkish Airlines, which flies five scheduled flights a week to Ercan via Antalya, Dalaman, Izmir and Istanbul. (*FLS Aerospace*)

Once passengers reach the rear of the terminal they are transported to the international satellite by a tracked transit system (TTS) or people mover. These automated trains, which cost over £30 million, run every few minutes. Two 1,300-metre elevated and tunnelled tracks are used to carry a maximum of eighty passengers per train to and from their destinations. (*BAA Stansted via In Press*)

The panoramic view from the control tower as a KLM Fokker 100 slows down on the runway. In the foreground a Ryanair 'logo-jet', sponsored by Hertz Rent-A-Car, taxies eastward towards the terminal satellites. In the background is the long-term aircraft parking area, with two L1011 TriStars and an HS.Trident used for training purposes. (*Author*)

Airbus A320-231, registration G-OOAE, operated by charter airline Air 2000, taxies into the international satellite on a murky day in 1999. Air 2000, which uses the callsign 'Jetset', operates to over twenty holiday destinations from Stansted. In the foreground is a Fokker F.27 operated by cargo specialists Channel Express. (*Author*)

The baggage reclaim area, as with the rest of the airport, was designed as a clean, spacious and light environment. This contrasts favourably with many other airports around Europe that have expanded on a more ad hoc basis. The terminal is lit naturally via the roof canopies and the arrival facilities are situated on the same floor as departures, separated only by segregating walls. (*Dennis Gilbert via Foster and Partners*)

British World Airlines (BWA) operates a fleet of four BAC 1-11s from Stansted as part of their specialist charter operations. Previously known as Silver City Airways and later as British Air Ferries, BWA can trace their roots back to 1946. The future of the 1-11 seems to be in doubt: new European noise restrictions come into place in 2002, and expensive hush-kits for the engines may prove financially unsound for airliners reaching the autumn of their operational lives, particularly in the light of BWA's order for three new Boeing 737-300s. (*British World Airlines*)

In 1998 Ryanair used six of its fleet as 'logo-jets' – mobile advertising hoardings. The Boeing 737-200s could be seen at Ryanair's UK hub at Stansted in all their glory, painted in the colours of Kilkenny Beer (above), Jaguar Cars, Eirecell, Tipperary Water, the *Sun* and Hertz Car Rental. Ryanair began to take delivery of twenty-five 737-800s in March 1999 and now fly to new destinations, including Frankfurt and Turin, as part of their on-going expansion. Their continued growth seems to mirror that of Stansted itself. (*Adam Rowden*)

Go Fly, the 'no frills' budget airline from British Airways, commenced services from its Stansted base on 22 May 1998 when its maiden flight departed to Rome's Ciampino airport. The business expanded rapidly, and only eighteen months later Go Fly had increased its fleet of individually liveried Boeing 737 aircraft to thirteen. Go Fly, along with the new breed of 'budget' airlines, will clearly have an important role to play at Stansted in forthcoming years. (*Go via Cohn & Wolfe*)

ATR.42 of Newcastle upon Tyne-based airline Gill Airways taxies out to the runway hold-point. Until recently Gill used to fly to Newcastle and Paris from London Stansted on behalf of Air UK. Now the airline can mainly be seen at the airport during nocturnal Royal Mail services. (*Richard Parker*)

An unwelcome visitor! This hot air balloon somehow drifted into Stansted's airspace during a pleasure flight in early 1999. The balloon was a major nuisance for several minutes, causing disruption to regular airport movements owing to the infringement of air traffic control safety regulations. (*Richard Parker*)

An El Al Boeing 767 gets an assisted 'push back' from its jetty. El Al first used Stansted in 1978. Today El Al supplements its Heathrow flights to Israel with a regular Tel Aviv–Stansted schedule. This aircraft is seen in the airline's latest colour scheme. (*Richard Parker*)

There was another first for London Stansted when this Air France Concorde visited on a charter flight on behalf of the communications company Motorola. Stansted is the only UK airport, other than London Heathrow, which the French Concorde has visited. (*Richard Parker*)

The new air traffic control (ATC) tower has an unsurpassed vantage point from over 200ft up on the south side of the airport. The tower became operational in 1996 and is currently the tallest ATC tower in the UK. Aircraft movements, formerly monitored by radar situated in the airport's old wartime tower, are now under the control of the London Air Traffic Control Centre in West Drayton. (*Author*)

Aer Lingus Commuter operates six scheduled services each day from London Stansted to Dublin using their fleet of BAE 146 300s, but a total re-evaluation of this route will see them depart Stansted for City airport in 2000. Here EI-CLY *St Eugene* is pushed back from its jetty prior to its late afternoon departure. One of Go Fly's ubiquitous Boeing 737s sits alongside on Apron A. (*Author*)

Advertising Martinair's '40 Years in the Air', this McDonnell-Douglas MD-11 Freighter glides toward the tarmac. The Dutch airline operates a scheduled cargo route between Stansted and Bogota, Colombia. (*Richard Parker*)

Virgin Express flies a daily service from Stansted to Brussels with its Boeing 737s. The entire fleet is Belgian-registered and they fly across Europe from Brussels to various destinations. Virgin Express also operates from Stansted to Shannon in Ireland. (*Richard Parker*)

The original road names from the USAAF years at Stansted still remain in today's Business Aviation area. They have a distinctly American flavour and provide a clue to the past usage of the airport. Three squadrons of the 344th BG had their hangars nearby on the northern side of the airfield. Stansted's social club is one of the few buildings which remain from this era. (*Author*)

The view towards the airport's international passenger satellite, May 1999. A TNT Worldwide BAe 146 sits in front of the cargo terminal, while Boeing 737s of Stansted regulars Go Fly and Ryanair are parked alongside their respective jetties. The glass-walled satellite lounges provide a pleasant, unconfined atmosphere for waiting passengers – as well as an excellent view across the airport. (*Author*)

Federal Express use the 200ft-long McDonnell-Douglas MD-11 Freighter as part of their Stansted cargo operations. The aircraft is pictured here in dramatic landing mode, but this is just one of an average of over 450 movements at Stansted each day. (*Adam Rowden*)

Along with widespread upgrades of all the facilities at the airport, Stansted's fire station was relocated adjacent to the new cargo area and the busy taxiways. The fire service operates Kronenburg Mac 8s and 11s. These 32 tonne fire-tenders can hold over 6,000 litres of water each; they can reach speeds of 75mph and accelerate from 0–50 in 15 seconds. Each costs around £300,000. (*Stansted Airport Fire Service*)

Although in the old days surplus aircraft were burned up to give the fire crews valuable training, today's fire service uses a specially designed mock-up airframe on which to learn and hone their skills. The mock-up cost in the region of £40,000. (*Stansted Airport Fire Service*)

Viewed from the fire station control room, this is Lufthansa Boeing 737-530 (D-ABIW) *Bad Nauheim* taxiing alongside the runway towards the international passenger satellite. Lufthansa is one of Stansted's 'flag carriers' and flies scheduled services from Frankfurt and Munich. In the background is the former north terminal apron's 'golf' stands, now used as a parking area. On the right can be seen the airport's fuel storage tanks. (*Author*)

A British Airways' Boeing 777-236 waits on a rain-soaked apron for fuelling. BA began to take delivery of the wide-bodied 777 late in the 1990s and its fleet will expand to include forty-five 777s in the coming years. Boeing offers the airliner to customers with a choice of engines from three different manufacturers, Rolls-Royce, Pratt & Whitney or General Electric. (*Richard Parker*)

Business Aviation has vastly increased now that the old terminal has been turned into an Esso Avitat Centre specifically catering for such needs. It is not uncommon to see important foreign government figures use these facilities. (*Richard Parker*)

Britannia operates over twenty weekly charter flights from Stansted to a variety of holiday destinations including the Mediterranean, Spain and the Canary Islands. Only weeks after this photograph was taken in 1999, Boeing 757 G-BYAG was involved in an incident at Gerona in Spain. Approaching in stormy conditions, it skidded off the runway, breaking the fuselage in two places. Luckily no one was killed. (*Author*)

KLM uk's check-in desk is one of eighty-four on the three islands in the departure concourse. Passengers can arrive at the airport by car – Stansted has over 8,000 long-stay spaces – or via the high-speed train link from London, which runs to a station built under the terminal. (*BAA Stansted via In Press*)

Despite its French registration, this Airbus A320 is operated by the Italian airline Volare. This aircraft was formerly G-UKLK of UK Leisure International and is seen here after her repaint at Stansted's Diamond hangar. (*Richard Parker*)

One of British Airways' recently purchased fleet of Avro RJ 100s, which use the airport for regional services to Waterford and Manchester. In 1997 BA controversially began to change its Union flag tail livery in favour of a series of different multi-national designs. This particular design is entitled 'Animals and Trees' and is from Botswana. (*Richard Parker*)

Stansted has become Britain's fourth busiest airport thanks to the impetus of the new terminal and facilities permitting the arrival of more scheduled services than ever before. Passenger numbers are expected to grow to over ten million in less than two years, making it the fastest growing airport in Britain. By July 1998 Stansted employed some eight thousand people in two hundred different companies. (*BAA via In Press*)

Buzz, a subsidiary of KLM uk, became the first new airline of the twenty-first century when their inaugural service departed Stansted on 4 January 2000. Buzz initially operated routes to Berlin, Dusseldorf, Paris, Milan and Vienna and is set to expand rapidly. The interestingly liveried fleet of Bae-146s and Boeing 737s will be an important part of Stansted's growing 'low cost' airline business. (*Buzz PR*)

Despite the increasing movement at the airport, Stansted remains London's designated 'hijack airport' owing to its being the quietest of the three main airports, as well as the outer areas of Stansted being secluded and distant from passenger activity. Following on the heels of a hijack of a Sudanese airliner in 1996, the new millennium saw Stansted in the headlines again after armed captors brought an Afghan Boeing 727 filled with passengers to England in February 2000. The drama lasted several days before a peaceful end was negotiated. (*Essex Chronicle Series*)

The airport's growth to accommodate twice the number of passengers will require an increase to four satellite lounges at a cost of over £30 million each, as well as an extension on either side of the terminal. This artist's impression will be a reality early in the new millennium. (*BAA Stansted via Williams Advertising*)

BIBLIOGRAPHY

Ambrose, Stephen E., *D-Day*, Simon & Schuster, 1994

Austin, Lambert D., *The 344th Bomb Group (M) History and Remembrances, World War Two*, Southern Heritage Press, 1996

Bowyer, Michael J.F., *Action Stations – Military Airfields of East Anglia 1939–45*, Patrick Stephens Ltd, 1979

Donne, M., *Above Us the Skies, The Story of BAA*, Good Books, 1991

Eastwood, A. and Roach, J., *Jet Airliner Production List* (Vols I and II), The Aviation Hobby Shop, 1997/8

Eastwood, A. and Roach, J., *Piston Engine Airliner Production List*, The Aviation Hobby Shop, 1996

Eastwood, A. and Roach, J., *Turbo Prop Airliner Production List*, The Aviation Hobby Shop, 1998

Eastwood, A., Mitchell, S., Richardson, D. and Roach J., *Airlines*, The Aviation Hobby Shop, 1999

Freeman, Roger A., *Airfields of the Ninth Then and Now*, After the Battle, 1991

Freeman, Roger A., *The Ninth Air Force in Colour*, Arms and Armour, 1995

Freeman, Roger A., *Raiding the Reich*, Arms and Armour, 1997

Hamlin, John F., *The Stansted Experience*, GMS Enterprises, 1997

Havener, J.K., *The Martin B-26 Marauder*, Southern Heritage Press, 1988

Jablonski, Edward, *America in the Air War*, Time-Life Books, 1989

Smith, Graham, *Essex Airfields in the Second World War*, Countryside Books

OTHER SOURCES

Aeroplane magazine (IPC Magazines)

Airliner World magazine (Key Publishing)

The *Daily Telegraph*

BAA London Stansted Press Information

Various Public Relations Briefing Packs

APPENDIX

London Terminal Passenger Traffic 1947–98 (Calendar Years)
*Passengers in '000s

Year	Heathrow	Gatwick	Stansted	Year	Heathrow	Gatwick	Stansted
1947	282	0	0	1982	26406	11154	300
1948	386	0	0	1983	26749	12477	342
1949	310	0	0	1984	29147	13954	527
1950	386	0	0	1985	31289	14883	514
1951	372	0	0	1986	31315	16309	545
1952	766	0	0	1987	34742	19373	712
1953	1205	0	54	1988	37525	20761	1045
1954	1724	0	53	1989	39611	21183	1322
1955	2655	29	52	1990	42647	21047	1154
1956	3026	Neg.	43	1991	40248	18690	1684
1957	2476	0	22	1992	44964	19842	2332
1958	3519	186 (Terminal		1993	47602	20065	2671
		opened)	20	1994	51362	21051	3258
1959	4012	368	17	1995	54107	22382	3890
1960	5270	470	59	1996	55723	24106	4811
1961	6060	804	91	1997	57808	26796	5367
1962	6812	1042	102	1998	60337	29034	6831
1963	8027	967	112				
1964	9298	1114	94				
1965	10491	1362	5		PREDICTIONS FOR FUTURE YEARS		
1966	11769	1616	9		(End of Financial Year)		
1967	12437	1956	14				
1968	13160	2063	147				
1969	14096	2994	219	Year	Heathrow	Gatwick	Stansted
1970	15415	3684	496	1999 (actual)	61000	29500	7400
1971	16175	4655	493	2000	62500	30800	9800
1972	18294	5309	309	2001	64000	32000	11200
1973	20329	5765	176	2002	65000	33000	12200
1974	20076	5120	199	2003	65500	34500	13200
1975	21295	5344	238	2004	65800	36000	14200
1976	23242	5715	268	2005	66100	37500	15400
1977	23386	6588	300	2006	66300	38500	16700
1978	26488	7761	317	2007	66500	39000	18100
1979	27979	8701	347	2008	70000	39500	19300
1980	27472	9707	275	2009	72500	40000	20600
1981	26401	10730	262	2010	75000	40500	21600

(Figures supplied by BAA/Forecasting and Statistics First Point)